To my family, friends, and all those facing life's challenges head on.

This is for you.

www.mascotbooks.com

As Many Reps As Possible

The author and publisher advise readers to take full responsibility for their safety and know their limits. Before practicing the skills described in this book, be sure that your equipment is well maintained, and do not take risks beyond your level of experience, aptitude, training, and comfort level.

CrossFit, Forging Elite Fitness, 3...2...1...Go!, Fittest on Earth and Sport of Fitness are trademarks of CrossFit, Inc. in the U.S. and/or other countries, whose endorsement or sponsorship is not to be implied.

For more information, please contact:
Mascot Books
620 Herndon Parkway, Suite 320
Herndon, VA 20170
info@mascotbooks.com

Library of Congress Control Number: 2018908642

CPSIA Code: PRBVG1118A
ISBN-13: 978-1-68401-981-6

Printed in the United States

AS MANY REPS AS
POSSIBLE

SUCCEEDING IN **COMPETITION, BUSINESS,** AND **LIFE**
BY MAKING THE MOST OF EVERY SINGLE MINUTE

JASON KHALIPA

CROSSFIT™ GAMES CHAMPION

CONTENTS

THE DAY THINGS CHANGED

I began working on this book in the fall of 2015. At the time, life was really good. I experienced some personal and professional success, and I felt strongly about what I wanted to say in regard to building a successful business, being an entrepreneur, and doing both while staying balanced—mentally, emotionally, and physically. My work and family life were firing on all cylinders. I felt like we had "it all."

Things changed suddenly on January 20, 2016.

It was a Wednesday, and we had taken our four-year-old daughter, Ava, to the doctor. She had been experiencing pains in her legs. At first, we thought these were growing pains, something every child experiences. But soon after she started to experience severe bruising that just didn't make sense. She'd also had a series of ear infections… bad ear infections. The doctor told us that one of the infections was the worst they'd ever seen. It was pretty ugly stuff. I started to think something was really wrong.

At around 2 p.m., the nurse drew blood for a test. They thought that Ava might have some sort of significant deficiency that was throwing her system out of whack, like a severe lack of iron. They put a rush on the samples and sent them to the lab.

While waiting for the results, we had gone back home. My wife, Ashley, was making dinner when the lab called at about 6 p.m. They reported that there was something "irregular in Ava's blood work," and that we should expect a callback shortly. This was not the kind of thing we wanted to hear.

Five minutes later, Ava's doctor called.

"You need to take Ava to the Stanford emergency room right now," he said.

That was all he told us, but the urgency in his voice told us to not hesitate. We didn't have to be told twice. Leaving our dinner on the counter, we made the nerve-wracking thirty-five-minute drive from our home in Los Gatos to Palo Alto.

Our initial thought was that the irregular blood work must have had something to do with that kind of significant deficiency and it needed to be addressed right away, but we were just guessing and hoping for the best...we were in the dark about what was actually going on.

We entered the hospital through the ER and were directed to an individual room for immunocompromised children. We were alone in quarantine—things started to get really heavy. I will never forget that first trip. Unfortunately, it's one that we would become very familiar with. A nurse led us to the room, and before she handed us off to other staff, she said something that took my wife and me off guard.

"There's one piece of advice that I have for you," she said. "I've seen a lot of things happen here, a lot of stories. Keep a date night for yourselves. You have to keep your relationship strong."

Ashley and I just looked at each other. *What the hell is that supposed to mean?* I thought. For a split second, I considered telling her off, but I held back. Her words slowly began to make sense. It was like she had seen couples like us pass through those rooms for years...

and she had. She knew we were in for one hell of a ride—after all, we wouldn't have been called in like this if it wasn't a big deal.

Soon enough, we would figure out what all this was about. My father-in-law, Jeff, joined us in the treatment room with Ava as soon as he could. We sat there for hours, until around 1 a.m., when a doctor came in. She told us that two more pathologists had looked at the blood test results and asked me if I wanted to step outside the room to talk about their findings. We went out into the hallway to speak privately.

"We're fairly certain your daughter has leukemia," the doctor said.

"Are you sure?" I asked.

"We're 99% sure."

More emotions hit me at that moment than I can accurately describe. I broke down and cried for a while in the hallway. As you can imagine, a thousand thoughts—mostly bad ones—went racing through my head. I wasn't an expert on cancer, but I knew it wasn't good. No one ever wants to receive a cancer diagnosis… especially for your four-year-old daughter.

I pulled myself together, went back into Ava's room, and shared the news with Ashley and her father. Ashley and I went back out into the hallway and cried together. After some time alone, we made a pact that after we told our families the news, we would not allow tears in front of Ava. No matter how badly we felt or how grave the situation may look…we would *always* be positive. To this day, after many surgeries, treatments, and hospital stays, we have held to that commitment.

We also made another pact: we were going to crush this thing. Starting that very moment. So, we went back into the room and got to work. We talked with Ava about the disease, and why we were at the hospital in the middle of the night. Because she was so young, she didn't know what words like "cancer" and "leukemia" meant, so it was up to us to explain it all. She's a smart kid, though, and she knew that something big was happening. Ashley and I were able to define the disease in a way that was honest, but also hopeful and positive. Ava had an illness that was going to take some hard work to treat, but we were all in it together.

I knew right then that everything I had been fortunate enough to accomplish in my life—in business, as a world champion athlete, as a person, and with the financial foundation we had put in place—had been preparing me for this challenge. This was the test. We had a strong family. We had good health insurance. Our company, NCFIT, a fitness startup, had become a thriving, successful business staffed by competent people I trusted. I knew that Matt Walker, our CFO, and the rest of our team could run the show while I shifted one-hundred percent of my focus to this new fight against leukemia.

Later that same night, I sent Matt this email:

From: Jason Khalipa
Date: Thursday, Jan 21, 2016 at 1:44 AM
Subject: New Path

I have never cried as much as I have tonight. It is with a tear in my eye that I say Ava has leukemia and I will be at Lucile Packard hospital for at least a month. Treatment starts today.

Until further notice I don't want to be involved in any business. Maybe this is a day, maybe a week, maybe 6 months. I don't know at this point.

Matt, perform all necessary duties. Until I say otherwise you are the acting president. Let's catch up when necessary on necessary items. Can you please draft up an email to all employees?

Let everyone know in the company that I don't want to talk about anything unless it's related to my daughter getting healthy.

Thank you,

Jason Khalipa

A lot changed that night, including my reason for writing this book. Originally, I wanted to counter some of the nonsense I saw in the business section of airport bookstores. Over the years, I had picked up books here and there on my travels—and I was always disappointed. These book promise reward without effort, and a successful future without planning and hard work. Some were very hypothetical, with no real substance; others were based on a particular case study and were too focused on something that didn't apply to me. I saw everything but the simple message that said, "Get out there and get to work!" So, I decided to write a book about working hard, nonsense-free.

But it's much more than that for me now. My *why* for writing this book, my fundamental motivation and reason, has changed. I have always wanted to win, always wanted to be successful—but I had no idea that one day our daughter would be diagnosed with leukemia. Now, I had to win. This terrible event forever shifted my perspective and gave me a deeper *why*.

Even though my *why* had changed, I noticed something interesting relating to my stronger purpose for writing this book. The key principles and lessons that had been a part of my personal journey—from being a drifting kid out of high school without a clear vision to a world-champion athlete with a family and a multimillion-dollar business built from the ground up—were lessons that had become the vital skills and foundation I would need for what was by far the greatest challenge I had encountered: my daughter's diagnosis. As I'm sure you can imagine, or perhaps know from personal experience, being a parent and dealing with this kind of situation as effectively as possible requires emotional mastery, discipline, endurance, the capacity for total focus, and much, much more. I did not have these skills at the beginning of my journey.

When I look back over my life, I truly believe that I had been working toward this confrontation with cancer the entire time. In high school, I had a lot of fun with my friends, and was never overly concerned about the future. I partied hard and spent weeks on end hanging out by the pool, doing nothing. It was almost too late when I saw that people around me were working hard and moving forward, while I was stuck in the same place.

But I learned valuable lessons from valuable people all the same. As an adult, I developed a skill set that allowed me to accomplish great things while still making family a priority. All the while, I had been practicing different pieces of the tool that would see me through the most difficult challenges I had ever faced. That tool is the AMRAP Mentality.

My entire experience has confirmed my belief that it's critical to have a strong *why* to guide the actions and directions we pursue in life. I am grateful every day that because I had incorporated the AMRAP Mentality into my life for so many years, I was ready to fight, not without fear or exhaustion or pain, but without being hampered by those things. In the end, it allowed me and my family to focus on one thing: getting Ava well. And I know that it can do the same for you, so that if the day ever comes when you are hit hard by life and knocked down the way we were…you stand right back up, more motivated than ever.

CHAPTER 1

A SET OF TOOLS TO SET YOU FREE

As I write these words, I am immensely grateful to have enjoyed success both as a professional athlete in the sport of CrossFit, and as the founder and owner of a company I deeply believe in, NCFIT. Best of all, I married my high-school sweetheart and we now have two beautiful children, Ava and Kaden. We are happy, and Ava is on the path to recovery from her leukemia diagnosis. That is how I measure success.

It's a good bet that how I turned out surprised a few people. And to be honest, their opinions may not have been too far off.

My best friends are the friends I've had since high school. They know me in a way that is unique. They remember what I was like all the way back in grade school—a good guy and loyal friend, who could also be kind of a jackass. I think that if you asked any of them then (even our CFO Matt…remember him?) about my chances of being as successful as I am, they would have given you pretty bad odds. Actually, they might have given me no chance at all! I certainly wasn't the most focused, driven student in school.

Who knows, maybe some of those airport books are right… maybe I'm an example of how a person just got really lucky. Got the girl, got some muscles, won a few important workouts, started a business, made some money, and so on. Or perhaps a better way to put it—and this is how I like to think of it—is that I am an example of how a person can wake up, work really hard, stay focused and consistent, and discover what he or she is actually capable of.

Discovering my potential, and then realizing it in myself, took some doing. The toolset I would need for success was not something I figured out immediately. Rather, there was an education involved that I was fortunate—or better yet, privileged—to go through. The toolset that I rely on every day of my life is a system I call the AMRAP Mentality. It's a combination of a few fundamental elements that I do my best to apply constantly and across the board. I'd like to introduce it to you as well.

WHAT IS AMRAP?

AMRAP is an acronym commonly used in the fitness industry that stands for: **A**s **M**any **R**eps **A**s **P**ossible. In brief, it's a circuit-type workout where a stopwatch tells you how long you have to work, but you determine how hard you work. Here's a quick example: push-ups on your floor for one minute—as many reps as possible, AMRAP one minute. If you can get more than forty, I'm impressed.

For over a decade I have pushed myself against the clock in workouts, and the desire to get the most out of each minute has laid the foundation for the AMRAP Mentality. At its core, the AMRAP Mentality is about achieving your goals, big and small, through focus, dedication, and hard work. Whether you're in the gym, at home, or at work, the AMRAP Mentality is a system that puts your thoughts, feelings, and actions into an alignment that allows you to get the best and most effective work done toward your goals.

The AMRAP Mentality is broken down into five parts:

- Know Your Why
- Focus On What You Can Control
- Work Hard
- Shift Gears
- Re-Evaluate

Think about the first time you rode a bicycle without training wheels. It took some serious effort, right? Before you could even think about going fast or far, you needed *focus*. The focus required to just remain upright on two wheels is key to beginning the task. Once you can focus on that, you can go around the block. That takes *hard work*. You may hit a rock along the way and the bike might threaten to spin out of control. So, you need to *shift gears* while continuously pedaling and staying focused on staying upright. And when you go up and down hills, you have to keep pedaling even when you shift—this is adjustment while continuing to keep up your effort.

This is how the AMRAP Mentality works—it demands focus, hard work, the ability to shift gears, and the ability to re-evaluate. Not just every other minute. Not just once an hour. *Every* minute… for as many reps as possible. At first, you have to give it a lot of thought and concentrate on each individual piece, but soon it becomes automatic.

As mentioned above, the acronym AMRAP is drawn from a particular type of workout. Get as many reps in as you can within a set time period. We know from experience and exercise science that the hard, searing, and focused training that comes with a well-executed workout may take only a few minutes of your time, but the physiological and hormonal impact is tremendous. AMRAP in particular is a specific kind of workout that, when performed correctly, gets a maximum effect for minimal time.

I'll talk you through an example to showcase the difference that using this structure provides.

Let's say your workout is ten push-ups, ten squats, and ten sit-ups. Do ten of each one time, and that makes for the completion of a round.

Now, imagine a trainer at a gym says, "Hey, why don't you go over to the mat and do some rounds of ten push-ups, ten squats, and ten sit-ups, and in a while I'll be over to check in on you." Well, even with the most basic physical conditioning, this isn't going to be a very challenging assignment. You may not even break a sweat. You could do a round, lie back on the mat for a couple of minutes, stretch, do another round, and go get a drink of water. A half hour could go by without much drama...or exercise. Go ahead and visit a conventional gym, and watch people drift from machine to machine in a similar manner. You tend to see a lot of this kind of half-hearted effort. It eats up a lot of time and often doesn't have a huge impact on your development.

But let's change the dynamics a little. Let's put you in a group. On the wall in front of the group is a big countdown clock. The trainer sets the clock to ten minutes and gives you an assignment... are you ready? Now the trainer says, "How many rounds of push-ups, squats, and sit-ups can you do in ten minutes? Whoever does the most, wins...and your job is to try to win. Also, some of you have done this before, so I want you to try to be better than the last time."

Oh crap. Yeah, that lump in your throat is real. Now you're not only competing against the group, you're competing against yourself as well. This is a whole different ball game. I bet you your next pay check that you do more rounds in the AMRAP-style workout.

This demands a lot from you, and it is effective because it challenges you. That said, you will only slow down your progress if you hurt yourself while pushing too hard. Having to recover from an injury or undo mistakes committed in haste will result in lost time…time that could be spent working towards your goals. No matter what, do your best to stay safe while employing the AMRAP Mentality during your workouts.

NOT JUST FOR THE GYM

Let's take a couple of steps back for a moment, so you can see how this applies beyond fitness. It's obvious that the AMRAP workout lives naturally in the gym. But what about outside the gym? What about the boardroom, the class room…and the hospital room?

It isn't hard to see how people from all walks of life can benefit from some version of this type of training. Another way to phrase the main idea might be, "performance on demand," or, "performance under pressure." Consider this brief office example: you are assigned a project in which you must produce an important sales presentation targeting a big potential client. Management was surprised that they were able to land this opportunity…and now you only have a few hours to do it! You need to AMRAP those slides! And just like the push-ups, you better not do them recklessly! You must act quickly but maintain control.

There are all sorts of high-pressure situations like this that happen in life. They happen in school, in relationships, and when launching a new business. But in every case, the basic principal of the AMRAP Mentality can be applied. And there's so much more!

Back to our workout example. Do you see how the clock on the wall transformed a fairly exercise routine into a competition? How much more work is going to get done in a mere ten minutes? How much sweat and discomfort? As anyone who has done their fair share of these workouts knows, even simple bodyweight exercises can become nightmarishly challenging when you go all out.

Consider the effect: it's easy to burn through twenty minutes by wandering around the gym, or swiping around on Facebook, or engaging in any other time waster that is at our fingertips on the Internet. But within the AMRAP Mentality—combining a deadline, a focused work goal, competition with others, and competition with yourself—it's astounding what you can accomplish in five, ten, or twenty minutes. Imagine an hour?

How do you perform under pressure? Do you procrastinate, or do you hone the skills to maximize your output? More importantly, how does one or the other move you toward or away from your goals and serving your purpose?

The AMRAP Mentality is what I have long counted on as an athlete and an entrepreneur. It's broken into five parts which I've outlined below:

1. KNOW YOUR WHY

Your why is the foundation and fuel of the AMRAP Mentality. Hard work and focus are the heart of it, but the *why* builds the base. This basic structure, in which we establish work capacity goals within small chunks of time and add the pressure of deadlines and competition, is a powerful tool. It makes focus not just a skill, but a necessity. Focus is automatic when you set up the right conditions. And having a strong *why* will help refine your focus.

Knowing what you want and why you want it fuels the entire process. Commitment to your why will propel you towards it like a heat-seeking missile. The AMRAP Mentality is a toolset for getting hard, serious work done well and done quickly, but if you aren't really sure why you are doing something or you really don't want it badly enough, it won't work. Without a strong why it is challenging to succeed.

I'll give you an example in which I have some experience. If your goal is to become a CrossFit Games champion—great, I love it! That's a great goal that demands years of hard, focused work and stressful competition. Are you ready to give up nearly everything in your life to win? Are you ready to train early, train late, train sick, train on vacation, train on holidays? Does it pull at your soul when you're not training? Does it make you ill that someone, somewhere is working harder than you? My point is that your why has to be so immense that you not only do all the hard, painful work, day after day, but are also willing to make sacrifices on a routine basis. If you don't have a strong why in place, one day you will find yourself in the middle of a severe workout or agony-filled competition, and a voice is going to start whispering in your head. *Why are you doing this to yourself? You don't really want this*, it will say. If you don't have an immediate, unshakable answer, then it's over. You have just lost.

The same principle applies to nearly *every* goal and challenge. A lot of what I learned about starting a business came from…well, starting a business! Any entrepreneur will tell you that the path toward success when building a new business is never a smooth one. It demands around-the-clock work and attention. There are no days off. But there are constant lessons. You have to be willing to learn often and learn hard. Again, the source of your strength and focus, the fuel that powers your actions, is a strong why. For me, the why was a simple one: I had to succeed because I wanted to take care of my family. I had no other choice. Simply being able to put food on the table for my wife and kids and provide good health insurance were just a few of the many reasons I had to make it work.

2. FOCUS ON WHAT YOU CAN CONTROL

When you have a strong why and choose meaningful goals to pursue, you will eventually need to develop skills that keep your attention on the things within your control. Without being able to identify what you can control, you can become your worst enemy. If you're not careful, your mind will draw you into areas that you *can't* control. Left undisciplined—and I speak from experience on this—the imagination can come up with all sorts of things for you to fret about. You will quickly find yourself facing a black hole.

To achieve next-level focus, you must tune out the noise of things you can't control and dial in to what really matters. Guess what sorts of people tend to worry about things they can't control? People who often lose.

Think about it this way. Imagine you are back in high school biology class. It's time for the midterm. What can you control? You have complete control over your preparation, your mental state, your attitude, arrival time, whether you brought an extra pencil, whether you ate a good breakfast…you control all that and more. Now, what don't you control? You don't control the questions, the super smart kid next to you, how fast someone else finishes the test…you have no influence on any of those things. So why worry about them? If you get distracted by those things and end up worrying about them, you will likely have a less than stellar outcome. Instead, focus on what you can control.

After my daughter's diagnosis, my ability as a father and as a professional to focus on what I could control was truly tested. I couldn't control when a blood test was going to come back—

but I could control whether my daughter had the blanket or toy that she wanted. It isn't easy to admit there are things outside our control, but we need to do it anyway. This step is where the AMRAP Mentality can help you hone your ability to identify the things you can affect and separate them from the things you can't. Before we can apply the next steps, we need to be able to fiercely and intelligently assess what we can control.

3. WORK HARD

Good ol' reliable, old-school hard work is the currency of the AMRAP Mentality. It's a blue-collar type of attitude. There's a job to be done—so do it. It's not about searching out secret hacks and shortcuts. It's about being focused and putting in your best effort to accomplish the things that need to be accomplished. There's no mystery about hard work. It's work and it's hard. The important thing to realize is that with a strong why, you will have the energy, determination, and reason to put in the daily hard work required to get where you want to go. When your why is right…the work is actually enjoyable and undeniably satisfying.

This isn't to say that the work won't be tough, and that you won't get discouraged. It is natural to have days where you feel less motivated than others. The trick on those days is to rely on your why, and on the momentum from the good days. Your bigger vision will power you, so that you continue to the necessary hard work. If you ever feel discouraged or overly tired, just takes a few days. Re-set and go back to your goals. Getting burnt out in the first few days of embracing the AMRAP Mentality will do you no good—you are in this for the long haul. In a way, that was what that nurse was telling us, way back on day one: take time for yourself. You will need it!

4. SWITCH GEARS

Being able to survey your progress and toggle between gears is the fourth key aspect of the AMRAP Mentality. I have found it almost impossible to remain truly focused on one thing for an entire day—your brain and body need time to recharge and switch things up. Just like how a bike or a car need to switch gears in certain circumstances, so too in our daily lives do we need to switch focuses throughout the day.

From family time to business time to workout time, switching between these gears keeps you focused and present. At work, be at work…at home, be at home with your family. Shift between gears and remain focused during that time, once the gear is shifted you are no longer worried about the past gear or future gear…focus is on the current gear. From my experience, most people have three gears. The first is maintaining good relationships with family and close friends; the second is aimed at some way to provide for yourself and your loved ones; and third is usually a hobby and/or passion to pursue.

These steps are intertwined, which I'm sure you noticed. For example, switching gears can be a great way to fight against discouragement, like we just talked about. Focus, our second aspect, is *essential* if we are going to switch between gears and continue to stay on task. It's a waste of energy to jump back and forth between things you can't control.

5. RE-EVALUATE

Throughout your life there will be moments when you need to re-evaluate. Particularly before or after a significant event like having a child, getting married, or losing or gaining a job. These moments are inevitable, and they are a great time to completely deconstruct your *why*.

Re-evaluating is about being methodical in paying attention to where you are in your life, what your values are, and how well you're being true to those values. It's my belief that by checking in with yourself in this way, you can avoid going off course. I'll talk about this later, but for me it was this re-evaluation that led to the decision that I had to let go of competing as a professional athlete and focus elsewhere.

By taking time to think about where I was in life and reflecting on my responsibilities, I realized that my priorities had to be my family and rapidly growing business. It was not realistic to expect that I could perform well across the board. I could not win the CrossFit Games, build a global business, and keep my family together. Others might be able to; however, I knew I could not. When I made this evaluation, I also realized that I had finally matured. I was ready for a different challenge in life, and ready to enter a new phase—one less demanding physically but challenging and fulfilling in its own way. That's why re-evaluating is an invaluable part of the AMRAP Mentality.

MAKING THE JUMP

Let's jump into this. We've gone over the basics of AMRAP-style workouts and familiarized ourselves with the cornerstone of the AMRAP Mentality: knowing your *why*. This is the critical piece of my approach, and I urge you examine your own why throughout the time you spend reading this book.

My hope is that you walk away from each chapter armed with one more actionable item that you can apply directly to your own life. It doesn't matter if your goals are personal or professional. The

AMRAP Mentality will teach you that no matter your goal, every decision is an opportunity crucial to your pursuit of success. Similarly, it doesn't matter if you're just starting your journey or already well on your way. The AMRAP Mentality will guide you along the path you're supposed to be on. No matter if you've never done a push-up, never worn a tie, or never stepped into the arena—the time is now.

I am excited to share the entire AMRAP Mentality with you, and some of the many stories from my life that helped develop it. Financially, professionally, emotionally, and personally, we are going to turn you into an independent force, ready for any curveball life might throw your way. And with that, let's get to it. My own path in understanding and becoming proficient in the AMRAP Mentality began with a sort of wakeup call, one that led to me knowing and embracing a stronger purpose…

READER EXERCISE

Mindfulness AMRAP – 10 minutes:

Set a clock for ten minutes. Write down three things that you either have always wanted to achieve, have been putting off, or have tried to achieve but fallen short. As you will find out later, AMRAP is a scalable system; don't be afraid to start small if you have to.

Once you have your list, try to identify based on what you have read so far the step of the AMRAP Mentality that might have been helpful in achieving greater success.

Physical AMRAP – 6 minutes:

Set a clock for six minutes and do as many burpees as possible in the allotted time.

To perform a burpee, start by standing straight up. Drop to the ground so that your knees and chest touch the ground. Once you have touched the ground, stand (or jump) back up. To complete the rep, jump and clap your hands above your head. Every time you clap, count one rep. Ready? Go!

Jason's Pro-Tip: If you are just starting out your fitness journey, simply crawl down to the ground and then crawl back up. Take this at whatever pace is manageable. If you are more advanced, try to increase the speed of your drop, jump, and clap. Start fast and try to hold on!

CHAPTER 2

UNLOCK YOUR WHY AND BUILD A PERSONAL POWERHOUSE

I didn't just cook up the AMRAP Mentality for the purposes of writing this book. Rather, it's something that took shape over a period of years, as I did my best to be a better husband, father, athlete, and business owner. The AMRAP Mentality is a simple system based on knowing *what* you want, and even more critically, *why* you want it.

Your *why* is the starting point of the AMRAP Mentality. It is a source of energy, and your driving passion in the long, difficult road ahead. It's also your value structure and your code, which will help inform your decisions and guide your actions, both big and small.

THE SEARCH

Discovering your why is a big deal—it's life changing. This might be easy for some people; their why might be obvious. For others, uncovering their true why may be a lifelong journey (and for some a struggle). If you find yourself searching for your why— that's okay, as long as you stay genuinely invested in the search and don't just wander off aimlessly because you're afraid of commitment or afraid of failure.

If you are having trouble finding your why, don't get frustrated. You have already gotten past the first step, which is to be self-aware enough to identify you don't currently have a strong why—and even more critically…that you need one. The process of finding your why is one of reflection and learning to understand the bigger picture.

The next step is to realize that you aren't as in touch as you should be. In many ways, the journey toward your why is one of self-discovery. Be vulnerable while searching for your why, and accept that it might not come immediately or easily. And remember that sometimes your why might be bigger than you had originally thought. For example, I've already talked about why I wrote this book. But a bigger why for the book would be to support families going through pediatric cancer, which you will find out more about later in this book.

Your journey toward finding your why will eventually define your why. The way becomes the why (and vice versa). This isn't to say you should rest easy and stop trying as hard as you can when you discover your why. At that point, the real work is just starting! But if you think you can just get by working as hard as you can without any particular direction…you are wrong, my friend. This is a recipe for recklessness and eventual (and inevitable) disaster. No matter what, without your why or without the journey toward your why, the energy needed to focus and the capacity for hard work are not going to be there for you long…if at all. You must identify your why.

IDENTIFYING YOUR WHY

So how do you go about identifying your why? Where does this relentless drive come from? Are some people "just born with it"?

Maybe a lucky few know their why from day one. I was not one of these lucky few. In fact, I don't think this is something you can really be born with…at least not the type of why I am talking about. Knowing your deepest purpose is like paying attention to yourself in a very honest and sincere way. You might figure some of that out early on, but there is still work required. There are some people who are incredibly gifted in this way—they are keenly self-aware. And then there are guys like me, who needed a kick in the head to wake up.

The day I started down the path toward understanding my why and living the AMRAP Mentality was my first day of college. Before that day, I wouldn't have characterized the way I had been living my life as very purpose-driven. I had dabbled in some ill-conceived business plans, half-heartedly played sports in high school, worked part-time at the gym, and had a good group of friends I liked to party with. I also had a good group of parties that I liked to be friends with (see what I did there?). In all seriousness, I wasn't dedicated to any single purpose, but there was one thing I did take extremely seriously. My then-girlfriend and high school sweetheart, Ashley. As would happen in many other moments in my life, Ashley was surely the reason why that first day of college ended up being so significant.

West Valley College is a community college located about twenty minutes southwest of downtown San Jose. Despite being a largely commuter school, it's actually a very pretty campus—143 acres in the rolling foothills of the Santa Cruz Mountains.

Despite the serene campus, West Valley wasn't where I wanted to go to school. Ashley and most of my friends were going to Santa Clara University. Dating Ashley obviously meant I wanted to go to Santa Clara as well, but I wasn't accepted because of my poor grades. Even though I'd been accepted to a few other schools, I opted to go the junior college route, so I could eventually meet back up with Ashley and the crew at Santa Clara U.

Back to my first day at West Valley…let's just say the whole thing was a humbling experience. To be honest, I was a little embarrassed to be there. Not that I was above West Valley, but that I had wasted a lot of my time, talent, and energy, and I had fallen short of my potential.

The high school atmosphere that I loved was gone. High school had been about chest bumps, high fives, and having fun. There was built-in structure, and you didn't have to think too much about it. I made the structure work for me, and it didn't take a lot of effort. I coasted, and all the way from timid freshman to school-ruling senior, I found a way to work the system. I did just enough to get by. I played sports because I had some natural size and athleticism. I hung out with my friends during the day, and we partied hard on weekends. Come Monday, I showed up to the classes I knew I needed to attend and skipped the ones I knew I could. Signed, sealed, delivered—I graduated. Sounds familiar, right?

When I sat down for my first core curriculum class at West Valley, the differences between my high school life and life in community college started to sink in. I didn't know anyone in the class, and it sent me into a bit of a spiral. I found myself in a big lecture hall with people of all ages and backgrounds. I looked around the room for a familiar face, but all I could see and feel was change…a radical shift from everything I had known. My heart rate spiked, and I was scared.

We were asked to introduce ourselves to the class. One by one students stood up, gave their names, and offered up a personal detail or two. People were in that room for all sorts of different reasons, and they came from all walks of life.

There was a woman sitting next to me who looked like she was in her early twenties. I looked at her as she stood, hoping to establish some unspoken common ground with someone. It didn't turn out that way. I can't remember her name, but when she told the class, "This is my seventh year here," my heart nearly stopped.

Seventh year. SEVENTH YEAR!?

When my turn arrived, I stood up, looked around the room, and somehow managed to say, "I'm Jason. This is my first semester." Then I sat back down. I was freaked out. My mind spun with images of a murky, aimless future. I had trouble concentrating for the rest of the hour. White, muffled noise was all I could hear (kind of like the teacher in Charlie Brown cartoons). This woman was in her seventh year of community college. Wasn't the idea to get an associate degree in two years and then move on to a full-time job or transfer to a four-year university?

I started to wonder if I was on track to do the same thing. Was I bound to end up like the person sitting next to me—stalled out in school for seven years? Was it even remotely possible that I could sink into the same sort of comfort zone and aimlessly keep taking community college classes while watching almost a decade of my life fade away?

When the class ended, I couldn't get out of the room fast enough. I had to figure out what I was going to do with my life that very day. The things I didn't want in life came into sharp focus first. I didn't want aimlessness, uncertainty, fear, or laziness. I wanted purpose, investment, diligence, and grit. This experience literally moved me. I would soon go from not having a strong why at all to having life-altering, soul-guiding why. Things were about to change fast.

I began to reflect in a way that I never had before—brutal honesty. Because I hadn't taken high school seriously, I had unconsciously created a division between some of my friends and me. Many of my peers had moved on without me. And they should have! But in that moment, two words changed me forever—seventh year. Maybe I was so disturbed by the fact that you could blink and be in your mid to late twenties with little to no progress. Maybe it was because I had begun to realize that much of my "success" to date (graduating high school) was only the result of a system and structure that had done all the work for me—you literally had to try to fail. Perhaps most accurately and honestly, I wondered if I actually had more in common with the woman on the seven-year-plan than I could admit.

My shock deepened as I realized an additional fact about community college…no one cared whether I drifted or not. I could skip class, drop out, whatever. The structure that had pushed me through high school was gone. It was all up to me now. For the second time in not so many hours, I was really scared. But this time, something burned inside me that was stronger than my own fear. All I could hear in my own head was the word "GO." So, I went.

This was the moment my why began to take shape and grabbed hold of me, and in a certain way, took over. My why manifested in two ways. First, would Ashley ever want to be with someone as lost and unmotivated as I had been? And second, would I be able to live with myself as a seventh-year freshman?

Gripped by these thoughts, I raced to the admissions and counseling building. I signed up for an immediate appointment and waited my turn. The ink from the notes of my first class probably hadn't dried yet. After what seemed like an eternity, they called me in to the office.

The counselor's room was small, which made my anxiety even more pronounced. I got right down to business and launched into it before even sitting down.

"I need to get the hell out of here as fast as I can."

I paused momentarily, almost in shock at my own words. The counselor blinked at me. When I think back to that day now, I realize that she had probably seen people like me all the time. People freaking out on the first day, just dying to get out. There was a brief silence. I didn't know whether the counselor would throw me out of her office or laugh my words off as first day jitters. So, I continued, "Yeah, I need to get this done and fast…how do I do that?"

The counselor did her best to work with me, and I came out of the meeting with an understanding that I would have to take a full course load each semester and take classes in the summer as well. I was ready. And now that I had the necessary information, I wasn't going to waste time and find myself in that same office a year later having the same conversation.

Just GO!

TAKING ACTION

That day, I first discovered how a why could force me into action. After getting blown away by my first class, I stopped looking at school as a place to have fun with friends. School was work. School was a mission. I now had purpose…and I gave myself a deadline.

I don't judge people at all if they decide to go to college or not. But if you're going to college or considering any heavy investment in your education, you need to get the job done. If you're doing two years at a community school, just get in and get out. If you're in school to become a doctor, then buckle up for the next seven years…you've got to be in it for the long haul. If you decide to do something else entirely, like learn a trade or go into business for yourself, then go for it. But whatever you do, treat it like a mission. Go in it with a purpose. Don't get stuck in a rut, accumulating debt and using college as a comfortable place to drift around. Don't get a degree in partying.

There was a lot I didn't know, and a lot I needed to know. I had failed to pick up some necessary skills in high school when I'd had the chance. I didn't know how to study effectively, manage my time, or create opportunities. I was unclear on how to navigate the shift from high school jock to community college...let alone eventually to a four-year university.

I needed more help than the academic counselor could offer. So, I sought out mentors and experts everywhere I could. I asked for advice from people who had the right expertise and experience. I talked to tutors and professors and advisors both in and out of West Valley. I pestered the Santa Clara University admissions office on their expectations for applicants. I entered extracurricular programs at school to pick up missing skills.

I swallowed my ego, and I asked for help. The counselors showed me how I could accelerate my progress through the academic curriculum. I took the maximum number of classes each semester, squeezed in additional classes during the short winter terms, and took more classes during the summer. I had a plan, and I executed it with precision.

REJECTION: THE ULTIMATE MOTIVATOR

This period of my life is where my why started to shape every decision I made and influenced how I spent my time. If I was going to get out of school as soon as possible, I was going to have to co-ordinate my schedule for maximum efficiency. So, I took classes in the morning, carved out time to workout at 2 p.m., sold gym memberships at a local gym in the mid-afternoon, and left evenings for homework, studying, and dates with Ashley. I needed to work at all times to keep everything together. My day was packed—and I loved it.

I applied to transfer to Santa Clara every chance I got. I was completely wound up in the idea of getting closer to Ashley. After six months at West Valley, I applied and was rejected. A few months later, rejected again. Good, I thought, now I just want it even more! I wanted it so badly that getting another rejection letter after turning myself around and working hard to get good grades only forced me to work harder.

It wasn't until my third (okay, technically my fourth) application—after doing the work necessary to essentially erase the weakness of my high school transcript—that I got in to Santa Clara. I had reached my first goal.

These months spent at West Valley taught me many things, and even thinking back on it now, I still learn from the experience. One of the main lessons in all of this involves evaluating myself with honesty. The truth was that, even though six solid months of good grades at a community college was a fine start, my efforts fell far short of eclipsing years of poor performance in high school. I can look back now and laugh—did I really think six months would be enough?

The reality was, I had a debt to pay off. The years of sitting on my hands added up, and I was "in the red." There was no shortcut around it. It was a good lesson. You have to be honest about the work you need to do to go where you want to go. This is a brutal and harsh honesty. The kind where if you really think about it, the scarier it seems. But that's how you know it's right. More than just honesty, you have to be persistent with the work and not allow a setback—like getting a rejection letter—to slow you down. You want something bad enough? Okay, I get that… now, prove it. You have every opportunity to change your destiny with every choice you make. So, here's your chance…start with your very next decision.

ALIGNMENT OF YOUR WHY AND YOUR VALUES

As my why came into focus, several things started to happen for me all at once. This universal shift wasn't just a coincidence. Whether I knew it or not at the time, my why was clarifying my life goals, who I was, and what I stood for.

As I mentioned earlier, some of the most effective physical training produces a tremendous amount of hard work within a short period of time. I learned from this impactful process in the gym and applied it to other areas of my life. To this day, I do almost all of my workouts against a stopwatch. If you ask me to work out… you better believe we are going "for time."

College became a similar pursuit. It was "for time." My results really started to cook when I added the element of competition. I tried to think of academic classes in a group setting as a competitive endeavor. Soon, the why that had kicked me all the way to that counselor's office became stronger through action. It was taking shape and transforming from raw energy into a finely sharpened point. My why was like a voice, central to my thoughts, motivations, and actions.

I was burning up with a desire to succeed in school. As my effort in the classroom started to pay off, the desire to succeed in school morphed into the desire to succeed in business. I eventually came to the realization that if I wanted to achieve new levels of financial and personal freedom I would need to become my own boss. It was crystal clear to me that I would one day open my own business. I didn't know when or what, but I knew why.

My courtship of Ashley was eventually successful (though it may not have been the overnight success I was striving for). Like any young couple, we had our ups and downs. But transferring out of West Valley and proving to both myself and her that I was really invested paid off. Ashley and I were together, and we were happy. As our love and relationship grew, we knew we wanted a house, family, and life together.

In Silicon Valley, the real estate market can be pretty unforgiving, especially for first-time buyers. So, in order for us to get married and begin building our future, I needed to set my standards high when it came to income and saving. My resolve to reach my goals strengthened, and I tapped into a source of energy and drive that gave me the discipline to face the daily grind. After all, the grind was necessary if I wanted to achieve the things I really wanted.

WORKING OUT AND MOVING UP

I could tell, even in my early twenties, that this was just the beginning of my journey towards finding my why. For my why to have staying power, I would need to fuel it sufficiently for the long haul. It couldn't just be aligned with what I wanted in the moment; it had to be aligned with my core values. This is the stuff that really makes you tick. For me, core values are the two or three defining characteristics about yourself that are inalienable, non-negotiable. I value honesty, self-expression, and a real conection to my community. My passion and purpose needed to ladder into my core values. Did they?

Here's the thing…I knew I wanted to be successful and have a house, family, and all that. That was clear. It was also clear that I needed to make more money to do that. The tricky thing about money is that even though you need it, it can really mess you up. Pursuing it, obsessing over it, gaining it or losing it—these can all trip you up on the path to fighting for your why.

This is the reason your why needs to be bigger than simply, "I want to make a lot of money." In order for your why to drive you in the right direction, it needs to be soulful and in tune with your core values. If you're off track, you are potentially heading for disaster.

I have always been passionate about sport and fitness, and as my future goals began to solidify, I came to realize that my path would lead to owning my own gym. I was growing more intrigued by and engrossed with the power of fitness, and really enjoyed seeing people come in, get a great workout, and leave feeling accomplished. Seeing people work hard and achieve something is great, and I wanted to give that experience to others.

At the same time, however, I felt a sense of hollowness stemming from working at a conventional gym. For every person leaving feeling accomplished, I saw five people looking or feeling lost. I dug a little deeper and realized that there was an important piece missing. We weren't upholding our side of the bargain.

I was selling a bag of goods—long-term, contract-based memberships—and not a meaningful *experience*. These memberships weren't meant to invigorate and produce results, they were just empty vehicles. The fine print might as well have said, "We hope you pay on time and never show up" as the rep smiled, and the poor sucker signed the contract. Simply put, the conventional gym business wasn't delivering on the promise it had made to its customers.

Although selling conventional gym memberships earned me a nice commission check, most of the people I sold to ended up not getting much out of the gym. It generally went the same way…I would pitch the membership package, they would buy it, and in three weeks I'd never see them again. I was good at selling. Even though I could get people to buy them on the spot, there was no true substance behind their participation in the gym. They never really found a sustainable way to exercise.

At that time, it wasn't my job to ensure that. My job was to sell,

sell, sell. Eventually, though, it started to wear on me. I felt the burden of those empty promises. These people wanted to change their lives enough to buy a membership, but we weren't really giving them the tools to do so. Unless they had the support and mentoring they needed to cross the bridge into a health-and-fitness lifestyle, they would never make it to the gym regularly—even though they continued to be charged monthly for the membership. I was selling a vision of fitness that promised a new and improved life to members, but I wasn't helping them achieve that new level of fulfillment. I felt that at its core, this approach was deeply dishonest.

CROSSFIT

CrossFit is a fitness regimen developed by Greg Glassman. Cross-Fit is constantly varied functional movements performed at high intensity. All CrossFit workouts are based on functional movements, and these movements reflect the best aspects of gymnastics, weight-lifting, running, rowing, and more. Overall, the aim of CrossFit is to forge a broad, general, and inclusive fitness supported by measurable, observable, and repeatable results.

In the early 2000s, my buddy, Austin Begiebing, came across CrossFit online after his mom told him about it. Austin worked with me at the conventional gym and talked about CrossFit constantly. After a few weeks of cajoling I gave in and went with him to Union City, California. There, we met a coach named Freddy Camacho, one of the CrossFit "OGs," who put me through my first workout in 2007. It was brutal.

I thought I was in pretty good shape back then. I spent a good amount of time in the conventional gym and worked out long and hard. But that first CrossFit workout was something else. I remember I had to adjust the workout to fit a beginner. Midway,

I had to change the workout to jumping pull-ups (a scaled version of an unassisted pull-up), because I couldn't complete all of the regular ones. Even when doing something as simple as sit-ups it was obvious that I didn't have the same capacity as some of the men and women around me. Boy, did CrossFit intrigue me!

Austin and I played around with this new regime for a few months, cherry-picking workouts from the CrossFit website and trying out a few different places. After a few sessions with Austin, I began to appreciate the results I could get from these high-intensity, functional movements combined into gut-wrenching workouts. The workouts were hard, and I loved every second of it. It didn't take long before I was hooked. I was fascinated by CrossFit's ability to get more work done in less time…exactly the approach that had saved me in community college. Seeing the potential that Cross-Fit offered was inspiring, even more so when I noticed the very different business model the program offered.

An essential component of CrossFit is the idea that its practitioners make up a community. This is where it differed from what I had experienced at regular gyms. Rather than a system of buyers and sellers of memberships, it provides a close-knit network of people who understand that they are all in this together. This amazing sense of community combined with sharing the experience of hard work is the true driver of CrossFit's amazing results.

CrossFit's community-based approach helps ensure a thriving and engaging atmosphere. Rather than have people sign up for a gym membership and then leave them on their own to figure it all out, CrossFit offers inclusivity and guidance through group classes led by qualified coaches. From day one, it offers newcomers support through coaching and community. Coaching and teaching are part of the daily experience. Both the coaches and the other members want you to succeed, and they hold you accountable for showing up. It's noticeable if you don't, and in most CrossFit gyms if you're absent for more than a few days, you usually get a phone call, email, or text. When you join, you are much less likely to fall through the cracks. The community provides a safety net of support.

In other words, CrossFit delivers on the promise of fitness in spades. It helps people improve their lives across multiple dimensions and lends them a community to back them up. Plus, its methodology is rooted in math and science. Without getting too geeky about the actual method of it all…CrossFit makes fitness measurable, observable, and repeatable. You can actually point to real data that shows you have improved—you are undeniably fitter. At this point, I knew this was for me. I could tell that the owners of CrossFit gyms went to bed at night knowing that they were truly helping people become healthy and fit. This new vision really appealed to me, and defined what I wanted out of a fitness business.

NCFIT

Even after discovering my passion for CrossFit, I still hadn't yet taken the leap of faith required to go into business for myself. The seed of entrepreneurship had been planted but was not in full bloom. I was still somewhat under the spell of a "traditional career" and the idea that simply making more money would get me more quickly to where I needed to be was alluring. So, for a little while I kept selling gym memberships, but also began looking for other, higher paying jobs. At this point, I was one foot in and one foot out, dreaming of my life the way I wanted it to be but too scared to do anything about it…a precarious place to be.

Eventually I settled on finding a job in the finance industry. Why? It seemed like a safe bet. And because finance = money…

logical, right? Little did I know at the time, this path was definitely not in alignment with my core values, and even worse, would pull me further away from my why. This is the spell of money, and it can be intoxicating.

I was nearing graduation from Santa Clara University in early 2008 and interviewing in the financial sector. A few early conversations with portfolio managers and bankers made me start to suspect this wasn't the life for me, but I was still lured in by the promise of financial success. They dressed in tailored suits, wore gold watches, and were always busy...very busy. They had money for sure, and they made that clear. But when it came down to it, they didn't seem to be like me and I didn't seem to be like them. We were different through and through. I still felt obligated to go through the motions, though. After all, my parents had spent a lot of money on my education, and I knew their expectation was that I would find a traditional job with a salary, benefits, and all that.

Despite my misgivings, I eventually scored a big-time interview with a local financial services company—exactly the kind of job I was "supposed to" get. I prepared well by studying the company and anticipating the kinds of questions the interviewer would ask. I neatly pressed my one and only suit and mentally prepared. I should mention that my suit wasn't really an actual "suit." Instead, it was a black blazer with a pair of black slacks. The blacks matched just well enough to the naked eye. I paired it with a collared shirt, spit-shined black loafers, and a tie I borrowed from my dad. He even helped me tie it. I thought I was sharply dressed.

I arrived early and was told by the receptionist to sit in the waiting area. She gave me a form to fill out. *Okay, this is pretty standard*, I thought. But scanning it, I realized they wanted me to write down the names and phone numbers of people who might make good customers for the company. Estimated income levels, best daytime contact, relationship to me…they wanted sales leads. My heart sank a little bit, and I uneasily filled out the application. Soon, I was called into a very neat, but also very sterile, office. It was stuffy, and the walls were adorned with stock paintings of nature scenes. It was kind of like the office next to it, and the one next to that one, and so on. Cookie cutter, rubber stamped. You know what I mean?

I greeted the interviewer with a smile, and she asked me to take a seat. I answered each question with enthusiasm and energy, and it went very well. She told me that I was a solid candidate for the job, and we began talking about my next interview, which would be with her manager. I was charged up! Maybe this wouldn't be so bad after all.

I stood up, thanked her, and gathered my things.

"By the way," she said as I was walking out the door, "for the next interview, you'll want to improve on the…suit."

Improve the suit? Say what? Her tone and message really caught me off-guard. To this day, I can still hear the self-importance in her voice.

The uneasy feeling I'd had when filling out the sales leads form returned with a vengeance. By the time I reached my car, I was downright angry. In the interviewer's world, the suit I was wearing was substandard and low-class. She thought I looked cheap and unprofessional. No, my suit wasn't custom fitted, but it was clean and carefully pressed. My shoes weren't Armani, but they were freshly shined. I was a twenty-two-year-old guy who had just spent four years grinding his way through college trying to look his best. I took a lot of pride in how I looked that day. She had really shot me down with a few careless words.

What really got to me was that despite all the care I had put into preparing, I had been judged not on my character but on how much my suit cost (or looked like it cost). The interviewer had made it clear that people at the company were going to calculate my value as a person based on how rich (or poor, in this case) my clothes made me look.

This woke me up, and the great wealth promised by a job in finance faded into the background. First off, did I really want to spend the rest of my life at work in a suit and tie? Was that what I wanted to be? Despite my best efforts, I had been told to come back looking sharper and better groomed for the next interview. What next interview, I thought.

I walked out of the office and climbed the steps to the third level of the parking garage. My future career felt like it was a blazing, four-alarm fire. Sirens were blaring in my head. This was no joke. It was a good opportunity for a business grad, and it was a smart, comfortable choice. Was I in any position to pass that up?

It was traditional and safe for sure. But was it me?

My heart said no, absolutely not. It was a resounding and echoing NO. This was 100% not me. First off, if my best dress wasn't good enough for them, then why bother? Besides, this wasn't how I felt comfortable either. If I were to define my ideal dress style, I would characterize it as, "clothes in which I can move around easily." Suits feel like straitjackets. However, attire wasn't the real problem. The problem was that I wanted to go into business for myself. I wanted to compete in the sport of business, and I wanted that business to be in a world which I was passionate about—fitness.

I wanted to be my own boss and feel comfortable in my own skin. I wanted to be in an industry where I would be judged not by the price of my suit, but by my work ethic and results.

The realization of my path poured over me. I was attracted to the uncertainty and discomfort of being an entrepreneur, not because of the risk and reward but because it would force me to push the boundaries of what I was capable of doing. Perhaps I could sense that it was a pivotal decision. I knew that if I pursued the financial services job, ten years could fly by, and I would regret that I hadn't taken the chance to do something greater. For all I knew, I could be the one sitting at that desk telling some recent grad to press his lapels better next time. I could never be that person and being true to myself was far too important to ignore.

The decision was made.

I'll never forget the call I made to my dad while walking to my car. I had never felt as sure of anything in my life as I did at that moment when I pulled out my cell phone and dialed. I knew that I needed to follow my passion—my why—and start my own business.

The phone rang a few times. I was nervous, as you can imagine, but not because I wasn't sure of my decision. That was certain. I just wasn't sure what my parents would say. It rang again, and he finally picked up:

"Jason, how did the interview go?"

"Hi, Dad. I have something to tell you...I want to wear gym shorts and a t-shirt to work every day. I want to improve people's lives. I want my hard work to be directly related to my success. I want to open my own gym."

It couldn't have been more than two or three seconds...

"Okay. Let's do it," he said.

HONORING YOUR WHY WITH ACTION

In June of 2008, I graduated from SCU. In July of the same year, I won the CrossFit Games and opened the doors of our business, NorCal CrossFit, which would become NCFIT. Neither task was easy, and I still had a lot to learn.

My parents have always been amazingly supportive of me, but

helping me go into business for myself was the culmination of that support. Although deep down I knew I always had their support, this particular time I could sense they were going all in with me… despite what they might feel was the safest play.

At first, my parents weren't entirely sold on the idea of me going into business for myself. But they wholeheartedly wanted what was best for me. A few conversations followed that fateful phone call, and we reached an understanding. In the end, I knew that I was making the right decision. The decision to open up my own business aligned squarely with my why and my core values. I knew that even if there was doubt from my friends and family about the risks, they would be there for me. It dawned on me that failure simply wasn't an option. If I wanted to stay true to my why, cultivate my core values, build a life with Ashley, make my parents proud, and prove to myself that I could do it all and more, then there was only one outcome…to win.

I've said it before, and I'll say it again: your why and your core values need to be in sync with one another. If they are not, there's a fatal flaw in the matrix. Your why and your core values need to support one another harmoniously, seamlessly. For me, the values of honesty, connection through community, and self-expression aligned perfectly with my why. However, when applied to selling empty promises through gym memberships or pushing paper as a financial analyst, there was a direct and massive conflict. It wasn't me. Could those opportunities have eventually helped me realize my why? Maybe. But I would have been one unhappy son of a gun for a very long time…I couldn't handle that type of stress. I had to be me.

So, I went into business for myself. It was go time.

To be honest, I didn't really know what I was getting into. There were certain things I knew for sure. I loved fitness. I wanted to work hard. I wanted to help others reach their goals. But taking those things I knew for sure and translating them into concrete steps that would lead me to my own gym was not easy. I figured I had the basics, and I would see what happened.

The first step to owning a gym business was finding the right location. After some searching, I found a 1,200-square-foot warehouse space in a small commercial park in Santa Clara. It wasn't perfect, but it would work. Now all I had to do was convince the landlord to rent his property to the twenty-two-year-old kid in a t-shirt and shorts who had never rented property before…

This took some work. I was full of passion and assurances that I would be successful, but I didn't have any collateral, which was what the owner of the property really wanted to see before agreeing to rent to me. After haggling back and forth for some weeks, I think he finally came to see my passion for the business. He agreed to rent me the building. I truly believe that he saw my drive and took a chance on me.

Even though I had been working hard for years, I still needed a loan from my parents to start the gym. For all intents and purposes, I was broke…which I'll explain in minute. But to my parents' credit, they continued to believe in me. They gladly offered up their credit card so that I could purchase $5,000 in equipment. I didn't enjoy asking for this loan, but it would allow me to start classes as soon as I took the keys to the warehouse.

MISADVENTURES IN BUSINESS

This is tough for me to talk about. I needed to borrow money from my parents because of several missteps that had left me with little cash in the bank. I'll take you through these missteps, because although they cost me money, the lessons learned in the process were invaluable and still serve me well today.

The first event in my costly education in business began back when I had just entered my teen years. When I was fourteen, I worked part time at a community center. Using the money I had saved there, I made my first investment at the bold age of sixteen. I thought I was a real slick investor…while working the front desk at a health club.

I put a total of $5,000 into a company that I thought was going to be a big hit. The company touted a revolutionary product called…The Batter Blaster. Other investors convinced me that this was a "cannot miss" opportunity. So, I pulled the trigger…$5,000 to support The Batter Blaster. That is a lot of money for a kid to put into anything, but that's how sure I was about The Batter Blaster.

The Batter Blaster was pancake mix in a can. It resembled a canister of whipped cream. You'd wake up in the morning, squeeze the batter into a pan, and cook it up—no measuring or mixing of ingredients required! Not only was it convenient, but the batter was organic as well. The company was seemingly on a rocket ride to the top. The product was already being sold at Costco, and it looked like the sky was the limit.

Well, the sky was not the limit. As it turned out, through a series of events beyond my control, I lost the entire $5,000 investment when the company folded a year or so later. I learned quite a bit from this experience. First, I learned that when it comes to investing (whether you are investing money, time, or energy), it is important not to get distracted by the shiny bells and whistles of something if the foundation is crumbling.

More importantly, though, this was my first life lesson on the second step of the AMRAP Mentality—focus on what you can control. Unfortunately, I didn't learn this lesson in its entirety until several years later, which brings me to my first foray into buying property…

I was nineteen at the time and had finally recovered financially from the pancake debacle. I was ready to try again. I took another shot at investing, this time in real estate—a much sounder bet, I reasoned. Can't go wrong with real estate, right? The deal put me and a few friends on the ground floor of some highly sought-after land—in a remote part of Idaho (writing this now, it's a little embarrassing). For a relatively small investment, we could potentially see huge returns. I did a little research and decided it made sense. I was able to put up $10,000 this time. My goals were strictly financial—invest the money in the real estate, sell it quickly, and rake in a huge profit. That was the idea anyway. Unfortunately, this project also went nowhere, and I lost the $10,000…every penny of it.

I was working hard at the time and making good money selling gym memberships. When word came back that the money was gone, my stomach turned so sour that I had to sit down. This loss stung. How could I miss *again*? And this time for $10,000! I look back on the Idaho land grab and realize failure had been all but inevitable. I knew nothing about real estate, and more importantly, I knew nothing about the real estate market in Idaho.

The deal had been too good to be true. What I've learned in business, and in life, is that if it seems way too good to be true… it probably is. I may as well have bought land on some booming new settlement on Mars or bought the deed to the Brooklyn Bridge from the guy on the corner selling fake Rolex watches.

These two experiences are great examples of learning to understand what you can control. I had no control at all over the decisions made by the owners of The Batter Blaster and some plot of land 2,000 miles away. I should have realized that early on and figured out that if my money was in the hands of someone I didn't know, far away, being allocated in any number of ways—well, then I had no chance.

These decisions were foolish on their own, and particularly so considering my net worth at the time. I should have invested in something I had more control over, and I should have taken more time to understand the leadership of the businesses I was getting involved with, rather than falling in love with a breakthrough technology in pancake mix.

So, for my third and final attempt at business, I went in the opposite direction. I would be in a position to control as much as possible, and only interact with leadership that I knew and understood. In this case, that would be my friends. Unfortunately, I overcorrected...

This third lesson came in college. Instead of investing in someone else's idea, my friends and I took it upon ourselves to pursue our own: the next big clothing brand. We named the company Faded Lifestyles. This was a project targeting the college-aged market, which had a proclivity for the nightlife and fashion.

After a long day of classes, training, and work selling memberships in the evening, I spent time on the new company. My friends and I hung out late into the night, working on our business plan. It was a lot of fun. This was at about the same time when the first hints of the AMRAP Mentality became apparent to me.

We gathered at our "company headquarters" (what we called "the shanty"—a two-bedroom apartment where a couple of my friends lived) and talked business. We built the company from the ground up, without knowing a thing about starting a business. We learned how to work with the municipality in getting the paperwork together. It was a banner day when we registered for business in Santa Clara County. Under "Owners," we listed our four names. I remember having to print as small as possible to make my signature fit within the allocated space.

A company with four young owners certainly had its challenges, but we worked extremely well together. In fact, we are all still good friends today. At Faded Lifestyles, we learned how to source clothing, work with vendors, and build grassroots awareness. We designed and executed a promotion plan, including going out to top area nightclubs to showcase our products. This was probably the highlight for the ownership team. We weren't yet twenty-one, but my cousin, who happened to be a club promoter, would get us a private table, get us on stage, and allow us to throw out Faded Lifestyles shirts into the crowd. It was one hell of a time. I was young, hungry, and fired up to sell some gear.

Increments of $5,000 seem to be my sweet spot, so that is what I put in at the outset. We worked at it for two years. But the initial investments dried up fast, and we kept shoveling more money into the business just to keep it going. We hoped the momentum would eventually kick in. In the end, Faded Lifestyles didn't turn a corner. It turned into another considerable investment that never made me any money. We were in over our heads and didn't know how to really run an apparel company, despite our undeniable passion for the brand. And after all, we were still full-time students!

There are a few takeaways from my experience with Faded Lifestyles. Even though I had the "focus on what you can control" part down, I didn't really implement a full understanding of the principle. While it is okay to start a business in an industry that you don't understand, it is *not* okay to not do your due diligence and actually learn the industry.

Due diligence in business, looked at through the lens of the AMRAP Mentality, is all about ensuring you have the appropriate amount of industry knowledge needed to succeed and are focusing on the things that matter. Invest in what you know and focus on what you can control. What are the things you can you control? You control effort. You control attitude. You control time management. You control fiscal responsibility. You control who you choose to work with and where you choose to sell your product. You control your level of preparation. But most importantly, you control your own actions and reactions.

To this day, I educate myself constantly on the fitness industry. I've also fought hard to make myself an expert in pediatric cancer. I attend seminars as often as possible about upcoming or emerging treatments and new breakthroughs. Knowing these things is an absolute priority for me and my family, and I want to be as knowledgeable as possible so that I can make informed decisions.

Faded Lifestyles really taught me about the principle of earned confidence. To this day, it still comes in handy for me. When you take on an important project that requires direct experience and knowledge that you don't have, preparation is the only solution. You have to prepare as thoroughly as possible, and part of that preparation is finding the right experts and mentors to draw upon for knowledge. That knowledge will enable you to avoid fatal errors—like the ones we made with Faded Lifestyles. You could have all the passion in the world, but if you don't apply that passion in a meaningful and productive way, you will go nowhere. That's why Faded Lifestyles never got off the ground. Passion without action is just wishful thinking.

WHEN YOU LOSE, YOU LEARN

All these lessons were now part of the business education that would guide me in the fitness industry. In opening my first gym, I was fortunate to have the earned confidence that came with years of working in a gym. I had interacted with hundreds of gym-goers, and had great mentors that helped me learn the ropes from the inside out. This earned confidence from hard-won preparation...I had learned everything I could about CrossFit and running a successful fitness business. This education, and the hard knocks I had received from my other experiments in business and investing, were invaluable to me. They were invaluable in the first class on the first day, and they remain so during the global expansion of NCFIT.

Most people can recognize the difference between earned and fake confidence. My first landlord certainly could tell the difference. He knew the scrappy twenty-two-year-old in front of him was confident and passionate, but he had to cover his ass too. He offered me a six-month lease. Six months is barely enough time to start seeing real results for clients, but I figured that in six months, I'd either be broke or doing well enough that we would need to move to a larger space. I picked up the pen and feverishly signed the lease. Then and there, on the hood of my first landlord's white pickup truck, NorCal CrossFit was born.

The clock was ticking. I knew in a few weeks the next rent check would be due. I went to work with no hesitation. An early version of the AMRAP Mentality kicked into gear. It told me, "Just *go*, Jason!" With my why as the energy source fueling this high-speed effort, I went HARD.

First, the old warehouse needed some love. The space was little more than four walls and some dust. I found some local guys to give the space some color. They may or may not have been gangsters—I can't say for sure—but they told me they would spray graffiti on the walls of the gym at no cost. I figured it was cheaper than paint. My family and friends helped me get the new space cleaned up and set up. When the paint dried and dust bunnies were collected, I unleashed my sales skills on the world. I'd talk to anyone who would listen about my new gym, and why they should join. If you were ever in line behind me at Starbucks, Subway, or Whole Foods…you probably heard my pitch.

I focused almost exclusively on selling in those first few weeks after signing the lease. As soon as we opened, I shifted my focus to giving my new clients the best coaching possible and building the best community for them. I was obsessed. If I wasn't coaching, I was interacting with the members. If I wasn't interacting with members, I was improving the gym. Rinse, wash, and repeat, over and over again.

Every second was precious. Everything I did had a sense of urgency. My why was incredibly strong, and I gave it my all. I didn't use life hacks. In some ways, it felt like life hacking hadn't been invented yet. It was just focused hard work. I knew what had to get done, and I worked hard at it.

As quickly as my other ventures had failed, my gym quickly became successful. It became clear I had made the right choice. Within months, the gym was so successful that we were able to move to a larger, better location. What I did in the early days of NorCal CrossFit was lay the groundwork for a shift ten years down the road, when NCFIT would become a global operation. "Work so hard that it's impossible to fail," was what mentors had taught me, and I intended to do exactly that. I think of that mantra to this day.

MAKE EVERY SECOND COUNT

At the same time, I was also laying the groundwork for a career as a professional athlete at the CrossFit Games. The Games have evolved a great deal since I started competing in 2008 and became the "World's Fittest Man" as CrossFit Games champion the same year. In 2008, the Games took place over two days at a California ranch. The weekend of the event, 300 competitors were organized into heats, and we competed in four very different, very grueling events. As it turns out, I would compete for the following seven years, and each year the event grew to new levels of grandeur and magnitude. During my tenure in the sport, the Games would move from the ranch to the sprawling sports complex now known as the StubHub Center in Carson, California. It went from hundreds of athletes gathering to hundreds of *thousands* of athletes entering the initial qualifying round, the CrossFit Open. Over the course of several months the elite competition is whittled down to the top forty men and forty women.

The CrossFit Games require athletes to spend a tremendous amount of time in what is lovingly known as the "pain cave." As a three-tiered competition that consumes half a year, there is no off season—if you want to win, you train all the time. Even if you're blessed with great athletic talent, accomplishing this requires spending a lot of time suffering through daily workouts that test your strengths, your weaknesses, and everything in between. For me, this meant getting up every single day before 6 a.m., hitting it insanely hard in my garage gym, and later on the same day pushing myself through the most rigorous workouts I could at NorCal CrossFit. All the while, I used the beginnings of the AMRAP Mentality to extract as much energy and effort out of my body as I could.

Oddly enough, when I won the CrossFit Games in 2008, the theme for the competition was "Every Second Counts." I had this phrase tagged on the wall in that first gym. When it went up, I didn't think of it as anything more than cool art. Little did I know that this phrase would become an important element of my mindset.

Every second counted when I spent those first days and weeks recruiting and training my first clients. Every second counted when I slept at the gym so I could work with new members at all hours. Every second counted when I acted as owner, coach, salesperson, accountant, and promoter. Every second counted that I got to spend with Ashley. At the end of my competitive career seven years later, I would hang up my sneakers as the 2008 Champion, and also be named the second and third fittest man in the world in 2013 and 2014, respectively. I tried my hardest to make every second count.

It's interesting to look back on the decisions we make in life. That single job interview was the proverbial fork in the road. What if I had gone on to the second interview instead of calling my dad? Would I have been offered a job? Would I have taken it? Maybe I would have realized that I was going against the grain of my why, and perhaps I would have eventually left to start a gym. But maybe I wouldn't have. Maybe I'd still be sitting behind a desk, prospecting different financial products, and doing something that only paid off in dollar bills. As it happens, being told I needed to wear a better suit snapped me into an earth-shattering state of self-awareness strong enough to jump-start my decision to rip off my tie and start my own business. It was my *why* that drove me to that point and continues to drive me to this day.

These are a few of the stories of how I formed my why, and what fueled my actions and changes in direction. If you take away nothing else from this book, I want you to realize that your why can be powerful enough to change absolutely everything and anything about your life. It starts with deeply knowing yourself and understanding what makes you tick. It starts with every decision, big and small. And it never ends. There is no finish line…only the next chance for victory. Your *why* flows from who you really are, the values you hold steadfast, and what you truly want. Your *why* dictates your focus. Your *why* provides the way.

READER EXERCISE

Mindfulness & Physical AMRAP – 30 minutes:

This exercise is designed to force you to think about your why. I was thrown into questioning my own by my experiences on the first day of community college, and that first interview. Rather than make fun of your suit, though, I am going to steer you through a timed workout.

Set a clock for thirty minutes and walk around your neighborhood block or your local track as many times as possible in those thirty minutes. You can walk, run, or jog. Just try to move the *entire* time for thirty minutes.

While you are on the move, think about your *why*. What do you want? Why do you want it? What does it mean to you?

If you get stuck, start identifying your core values, and then return to your why. Start with a big picture vision and the impact you want to have on yourself and others. Then, narrow it down to different silos in your life: family, friends, work, health, and fitness. Your why and core values should apply in some way to all categories.

Finally, think about what steps you can take today to start living your why. At the end of thirty minutes you should have at least two or three concrete steps you can take to start living your why.

CHAPTER 3

NEXT-LEVEL FOCUS

Focus is the second essential element of the AMRAP Mentality. After you define your why, your next order of business is to identify what you want to focus on. It's one thing to know what you want; it is another thing to go after it intelligently. My why is my family, our business, and fitness. Focusing intently on the task at hand while strategically and methodically fleecing away other distractions is key.

This is more complicated than you may think. Building the discipline to not pull out your smartphone at dinner is one thing. Figuring out how to balance your work life, professional life, family life, fitness, and emotional well-being—all the while achieving your goals in each and not letting one bleed too heavily into the other— is another beast entirely. As always with the AMRAP Mentality, there are several levels in any discussion about focus.

My family is undeniably my number one priority, but if I weren't trained and aware of myriad of distractions (worthy and unworthy) around me…they could easily slip away. Let me explain this point with one memory in particular that stands out.

It was early June in 2011. By all accounts, it was a gorgeous, Northern California summer day. The sun was shining, the birds were chirping…it was pretty classic. I was taking a walk in downtown Campbell, a suburb near my home with Ashley, and our infant daughter, Ava. I was present physically, but I was somewhere else mentally. I came back to reality right as Ashley asked me, "…I want to do it. So, what do you think?"

I realized that I hadn't been paying attention to a thing she was saying. *Do what? What do I think about what?* I was embarrassed. My focus was elsewhere. Not only was it elsewhere, it was non-existent…we could have been walking on the moon for all I noticed.

I remember the moment like it was yesterday. As Ashley was talking to me, I had actually been wondering whether I should swim later that day or not. Deeper down, I was guessing at whether the CrossFit Games would feature swimming that year. As I pictured myself in some sort of body of water, snapping on my goggles, my thoughts went something like this, *I wonder if they would ever take us in the middle of the ocean, have us jump off a boat, and swim back? That would be cool.*

At that moment, when I looked at Ashley and our baby girl in her stroller, I saw the disappointment in her eyes. I also realized that something needed to change, or I wouldn't be strolling around with a wife for much longer. My body was in one place, but my mind was somewhere far, far away.

DEALING WITH DISTRACTIONS – HOW TO HANDLE "THE NOISE"

This same type of distraction had happened when I should've been paying closer attention to my business pursuits. By the same year, 2011, NCFIT had begun to expand globally. As you might expect, I found myself in meeting after meeting. At one point, I was on conference calls with locations in Asia on a nightly basis for months on end. During meetings and conference calls, my mind would drift, and I would start thinking about my next workout—this was noise. I would start analyzing what weakness I needed to address in order to stand on top of the podium again as a Games champ. It wasn't the time or place for me to be thinking about barbells and burpees. But honestly, it was consuming me. There may not have been immediate consequences, but I could tell that if I let this go on, there would be. Then, more than ever, I needed to reflect and create some ground rules for myself. I needed to learn how to appropriately tune out the noise.

These moments of distraction were keeping me from being the best father, husband, athlete, and business owner I could be. I chose to write down the AMRAP Mentality on paper for the first time. I made a commitment then and there to follow this focus-based mentality. When I was training, I would think solely about training. When I was with my wife and kids, I would be 100% invested in them and our time together. When it was time to do business, I was committed to excelling as a businessman. I asked myself, no matter what I was working on, *Am I really going for as many reps as possible here? Am I getting in as much work as possible on this one task?*

This isn't to say that thinking about working out is wrong or less important than anything else. It's all about prioritizing and wisely applying your efforts. Depending on what you are trying to accomplish, an appropriate focus one day might be a distraction the next. Working out, family events, thinking about an upcoming business call...these are all very important, but don't need to be thought about or acted upon at the same time!

The ability to be really and truly present is a unique skill. Like any skill it takes time and practice to master. When you first start, you may find you can only stay fully present for short periods of time. Don't worry; we were all there at some point. But as your practice matures you will find the depths of your presence expand. You will begin to experience more, feel more, and appreciate more. The ability to be present without distraction is essential to mastering the AMRAP Mentality. It is also the piece of the mentality that I need to practice and remain aware of every single day.

NOT THE PAST, NOT THE FUTURE...NOW

Let me ask you a question...are we more productive today, or were we more productive in the mid-1900s? It's tough to say; however, I think it's fair to say that today we are more easily distracted. In the 50s and 60s, when people were at work...well, they were at work. There were no smartphones, video games, or social media apps to distract them. Sure, there were TV and other less advanced distractions, but the nature of our technology now revolves around constant access and incessant stimulation. If you have a smartphone in your pocket, you literally have a tool to go anywhere, see anything, or escape from any situation at the drop of a hat. I can't remember the last time I was at a restaurant and didn't see a couple sitting there enjoying a dinner together...on their phones.

Social media, email, texting, and the like are absolutely amazing, earth-changing tools. Of course, I'm not saying we shouldn't use them. We can and should take advantage of these technologies. The problem is that they often distract us from our actual lives, or hinder connections with the real people in front of us. This is undoubtedly detrimental, and you could argue may actually make us *less* productive instead of more productive. Utilizing the AMRAP Mentality has been my way of blocking out this kind of noise and remaining present with what I need to get done. Have you ever met someone who is always "extremely busy" but is actually the same person who never seems to get anything done? Detached. Distracted. Escapism. Distractions are everywhere. My challenge to you is to stay sharply focused and complete the task.

Of course, nothing will do the work for you. You need to both understand and implement focus. For example, these principles tell me that at times my phone is a distraction, but it is up to me to find the right way to deal with it and focus on the things that need to get done. So, for example, my wife and I will swap phones on occasion. That way, I don't have access to my email and social media, but if she (or anyone else) needs to contact me in an emergency, they still can. Little things like this aren't so little when they are done in a wider context.

Applying the focus element of the AMRAP Mentality is easy in theory, but in practice can actually be quite difficult—which is why I am constantly working on this skill. It boils down to the following: at work, be at work and *work*; at home, be at home and focus on your *home* life; and when you are working out, get after it and then move on to other things. The concept is simple, but the execution takes practice and constant reflection. Evaluate yourself with a brutal honesty. How present actually are you?

Recall the analogy of the AMRAP Mentality to riding a bike? Focus fits perfectly here. To ride a bike without toppling over, you must first master the balance of keeping yourself upright through intense focus. Have you ever been riding a bike, gotten distracted, and ended up going off course or even falling? It certainly has happened to me.

Just like riding a bike requires your attention and pedaling, the AMRAP Mentality demands your attention and work. And similarly to how you need to pump the pedals yourself, the work in your life won't be done for you unless *you* actually do it. Yes, this means YOU actually will need to roll up your sleeves, align your focus, and work. No one will do it for you, and you don't *want* someone doing it for you—because this is the path to unlocking your true potential.

One of the most crucial factors in developing next-level focus involves emotional control. The most critical error I see people make in business, competition, and relationships is the tendency to lose control of their emotions when the heat starts to rise or when they are faced with adversity. Winners stay calm and channel that stress into productive energy. Losers complain, fly off the handle, and lose their cool. In my experience, this comes down to a fault in focus. And it begs the question…are you focused on the right things? Or, do you tend to focus on the things that you can't control?

RELENTLESS POSITIVITY AND KNOWING WHAT'S IN YOUR CONTROL

Over the course of my career as a professional athlete, I've gone through many types of training. In addition to physical training, I've pushed myself to train up the mental muscles that help me get a handle on my ability to focus on the right thing at the right time, under the kind of pressure that a large crowd and live TV broadcast can stir up. To do this, I actually employed a mindset coach for many of my competitive years. This education helped me across the board to become less stressed, reactive, and distracted, and more focused, reasoned, and present.

In 2008, I was the world champion. But undeniably, my game was off during the 2009 CrossFit Games. I had become too focused on things that were outside my control, which resulted in a crippling anxiety that eventually caught up with me. Instead of focusing on my own preparation, mindset, and plan of attack, I was far too worried about my competitors, the workouts, the judges, and the conditions. There were several factors that caused me to lose my focus, but I'd say the biggest was that I hadn't learned to adjust to the pressure of being the champ, and to pressure in general.

By the time the events began, I had wasted so much energy on things I couldn't control that I had little left for the actual physical endeavor. These distractions took me off my game and likely caused me to perform less than my best. After coming to grips with failing to meet my expectations, and those of the people around me, I knew I needed to learn how to stay focused on what was in my control.

To that end, I met with mindset coach Adam Saucedo, who laid out the following exercise in which I charted the stressors in my life. Adam asked me to draw two circles on a piece of paper. He then instructed me to place everything within my control in the left circle and the things outside my control in the right circle. When I finished, it felt like someone had just taken a 500-pound barbell off my back. I had been carrying all this extra baggage for so long—I now felt free.

At the time, I did this exercise solely to help me compete; but later, I would incorporate it after Ava's diagnosis. While it didn't happen overnight, I began to more effectively compartmentalize what was in my control and what was not. I noticed the change first in fitness, and then in all aspects of my life. I worked for years on this single concept, continually attacking the mental image of those two circles.

It paid off in spades in sport, life, and business. When you are able to focus on what is in your control—and push away the things you can't change—you can turn almost any situation around. This is especially powerful during times of strife. Once you relinquish the worries associated with all the "noise," you reclaim power over your life. It gives me goosebumps to this day!

When working on this approach with Adam, I also developed the habit of incorporating positive self-talk. This took an especially long time for me to develop, but it played a critical role in so many situations. There were countless times when I would find myself in the middle of a workout and a negative thought would run through my head.

"Your legs are dead. You can't go much longer. You're finished."

"You can't keep up with him. You felt tired today. You've got so much going on."

"You're looking small today. The bar feels heavy. Your back feels tight."

Damn. Even writing those out makes me feel bad. Focusing on these types of negative thoughts will not help the situation—it will just let them get the better of you. Your legs won't feel better, they will feel *worse*. You won't snap out of it and get a burst of energy… you'll take a break, yawn, and feel even more tired. Sound familiar? These thoughts need to be treated like a cancer—identified and excised immediately. You need to force them out and replace them with positive reinforcement.

Instead of, "Jason, your legs hurt…" I shift the focus away from the pain and fatigue to sentiments that benefit me, like, "Woo! My legs are burning. It feels like they are growing. Good. Getting stronger." Sometimes I think of it as coaching someone. Those of you who have coached or motivated someone: you would never say something like, "Your legs hurt. You probably can't breathe. You shouldn't even be here." You would say, "Nice work! Keep moving! You're getting so strong! Your movement looks great!" And so on. This same thing should apply to the way you coach *yourself* through life. I use exercise as an example often because I truly believe the concepts of effective training transcend the gym and carry over into life.

COMMITTED TO CURING AVA

The development of these skills was really put to the test when Ava was diagnosed with leukemia in 2016. It was a situation that we obviously weren't expecting and one that demanded vigilant, maniacal focus from Ashley and me for an extended period of time. During that time, we came to rely on positive self-talk, focusing on what we could control, and emotional discipline that would enable us to make the choices necessary to cure Ava. It was the most important moment of my life. I could not be distracted by anything on the fringe. Sleepless nights at the hospital, emergency procedures, and being there for my family—I think this experience showcases the true power of the AMRAP Mentality.

When Ava was diagnosed, I called my mom and dad, Sue and Robert, immediately. My dad had leukemia when I was in high school and understood better than anyone else how to cope and get through this challenging time. Our families' unwavering support helped define and align my focus. This diagnosis, like it does for all when it comes to cancer, hit us hard. Everything was instantly turned upside down. Ashley and I were overcome by emotions, thoughts, and concerns. For example, what would we do with our two-year-old son, Kaden? We were likely going to be in the hospital for a month straight, and we needed help. I asked my parents if they could take care of Kaden while we figured out the path forward. I knew this would mean that my parents would need to take time off work and adjust their lives. My dad's answer will stick with me forever: "Your mom and I already told work that we will be out indefinitely. You need to focus on one thing—getting Ava well."

This lesson on focus from my dad was soon matched by the

rest of the family. Everyone arrived at the hospital shortly after the word was out, which is something my wife and I will never take for granted. Family is everything. When you feel like the room is closing in on you and you're grasping for the thinnest slivers of light…these are the people you need. I can only imagine what the doctors and nurses were thinking, seeing the waiting room filled every day for a month. I didn't take many pictures during this time, but I didn't need to because I'll never forget the love and support.

With the complete love and support of my family I was able to apply a supercharged version of the AMRAP Mentality to Ava's diagnosis. In a manner that could only be described as surgical, I systemically cut out things I had no control over and set my sights squarely on getting Ava well. The stakes couldn't have been any higher. I relied on the AMRAP Mentality to make every day, hour, and *minute* count as best I could. I relied on it to push myself to be better informed, better prepared, and better equipped. I read every book on cancer I could find. I learned everything I could about Acute Lymphoblastic Leukemia, or ALL. I leaned heavily on the AMRAP Mentality to evaluate the effectiveness of everything I was doing. I reevaluated my entire life. My focus was laser-like… nothing else mattered at this point but my family.

NEXT-LEVEL FOCUS IN ACTION

Let me take you back to Stanford Children's Hospital, but this time a few weeks after the initial diagnosis. By this time the harsh reality had set in—our daughter had cancer. My wife and I were keeping a twenty-four-hour watch on Ava, day after day. The slightest changes in her temperature or appearance were critical signs in understanding and identifying how she was doing. It was an emotional rollercoaster, with life and death hanging in the balance. It was exhausting mentally, physically, and emotionally. Day after day, hour after hour, we kept vigilant watch. The moments in competition, when my muscles burned and my entire body felt on the verge of collapse…they pale in comparison to those days. Our focus, stamina, and emotional control—all key elements of the AMRAP Mentality—were tested beyond what we could have ever imagined.

Then one day…we saw a shift. We noticed a very subtle change in Ava's vital signs, and without hesitation called the doctor in. Unfortunately, it quickly became clear this was not the good kind of shift. What had started very subtly turned into a sharp, severe drop in blood pressure. With a quick turn of his head, the doctor momentarily shifted his attention from Ava and looked at us. Even before he spoke, his eyes made clear to us the seriousness of the situation. His words were clear and direct, "If Ava's blood pressure doesn't come up in the next two minutes, I want to prepare you for what will happen. I will call a rapid response team. We will need to act without interference. It will be a lot of people." I gripped Ashley's hand firmly.

Two minutes later he called in the rapid response team, and twenty emergency medical clinicians rushed into the room. I've never been more frightened in my life. The lead doctor, to whom I will forever be grateful, spoke with clear yet undeniably urgent direction to the entire team. Each team member had a specific responsibility. It was the most inspiring expression of teamwork I have ever seen. Ashley and I could only stand back and watch. We held our breaths, not speaking a word. It was obvious that our daughter's life was not in our hands…but theirs. We quite simply, after all our watching and reading and waiting, had no control.

After what seemed like a lifetime of intense discussion followed by quick action, infusion, and medication, the tone changed. Ava was rolled out of the room and taken to the ICU. But the frantic pace had noticeably slowed…the tone went from life and death to one of optimistic concern. I remember looking at Ashley as we went upstairs and asking, "Did you hear how their voices changed?" She responded, "Yes, definitely." The whole situation only lasted ten minutes. But in that ten minutes we experienced nearly every human emotion possible.

I share this with you as a very cut and dry (albeit, extreme) example of what is under your control versus what is not. During those fateful ten minutes, it was clear that the only things Ashley and I could control were our emotions and mindsets. Literally everything else was out of our hands. All responsibility was squarely in the hands of Ava's doctors. Their actions, and God's will, would determine the outcome. My mind was occupied with other things at the time, but looking back I can clearly see that those doctors were using the AMRAP Mentality. They had a clear why (getting my daughter through this crisis), were focused on all the right things at the right time, worked incredibly hard, and when they had to, shifted gears. It was awe-inspiring to say the least. This is only one example of the caliber and professionalism of the medical team at Stanford. It wasn't the first time and wouldn't be the last that they saved our daughter's life.

ASHLEY – HER GRACE, HER STRENGTH, AND HER WHY

The AMRAP Mentality can be discovered and practiced in many ways. There is no one-size-fits-all solution. Some people might need many years (with plenty of mistakes along the way) to discover their why and develop the other elements. I certainly fall into that category—I was not an overnight success (and *still* don't feel like I have reached "success"), and the AMRAP Mentality is not something that, once achieved, stays with you no matter what! The lifestyle and ethos have to be maintained.

Other people, though, might stumble into their why, and learn the other steps of the Mentality, much more quickly. These sorts of people are often thrown into the deep end of life, knocked out of their comfort zones by something unexpected and difficult. My wife, Ashley, is one of these people.

When Ava got sick, Ashley's grit and positivity prevailed. As long as I had known her, she had been my rock. She was always consistent, solid, and thoughtful. She also encouraged me to up my game when I needed it. By the time of Ava's diagnosis, we had known each other for a long time. Ashley's actions and attitude in the hospital were certainly not a surprise to me, and I was incredibly proud. She didn't waste time or energy blaming anyone or obsessing over the question *why us?* She saddled up for the battle and took hold of what she could control.

Ashley has always been an incredible mother. But when we got Ava's diagnosis, I noticed an immediate change. She ramped things up into a higher gear, and I could tell she had found a new strength. I was all over the doctors, wanting to get additional information, learning about treatments, putting in that work. Ashley instantly became the one who kept everything running, with a level of commitment that never faltered. If a call needed to be made, she was on it. If something needed doing, she knew just what to do before anyone else had even processed it. What I saw that first night was an amazing thing. It had taken me years to find my why, but she had found hers in a single night: she was going to keep this family together no matter what.

At that moment, Ashley's words and actions were equivalent to a re-evaluation. I'll never forget the first talk we had after finding out Ava was diagnosed. To this day it remains the single greatest "pump up" speech I have ever heard. It was 1 a.m. when we received the news of Ava's diagnosis; prior to this we had a strong idea of what was going on but no confirmation. At the time it was Ashley, Ava, myself, and my father-in-law in the room. The doctor asked me to step outside and gave me the worst news I had ever received. It took me a little while to get myself together, but I finally walked back into the room to share the information with Ashley and my father-in-law. Ashley and I chose to leave the room and discuss in the hall where Ava couldn't see or hear us. At the time I was crying, she might have been also…emotions were high, and I was searching for the next step.

Similar to a warrior prepared for battle, Ashley spoke with clear and specific instructions.

"Jason, tell our family the news, tell them that if they want to cry they can cry outside; once they see Ava there will be no tears. There will be nothing but *positivity* surrounding our daughter. Let's go back inside…we will beat this."

Ashley led the charge emotionally. She learned right away the need to shift gears, to work hard—the AMRAP Mentality, in a way, came naturally to her. As Ava neared the end of her treatment, Ashley turned her why in a new direction. She had kept our family together, fighting as a unit against what life had thrown at us. Now, she was going to help other families do the same. To do that, she started a non-profit called Ava's Kitchen, which raises money to help other families battling pediatric cancer.

Ashley achieved a clarity of vision that I found truly inspiring. While we had taken different paths, and learned in our own ways, we ended up in the same place—the implementation of all levels of the AMRAP Mentality. The flexibility of this system means that it not only can it strike in many ways, it can also scale with any situation. You'll find out more about this later in the book.

READER EXERCISE

Mindfulness AMRAP – 10 minutes:

Set a clock for ten minutes and start with a blank sheet of paper. Draw two large circles on the paper. Over the circle on the right, write "Out of my control." Over the circle on the left, write "In my control." Before the clock starts, identify an area in your life that may be causing you stress. Whether it is work, business, competing, relationship, etc. Then start the clock. For ten minutes write down what is in vs. out of your control in the respective circles. The out-of-control circle may fill up fast while the in-control circle may only have a few items. Don't worry, that's normal. The lesson is in the identification process. Once you are done, look at the lists and start to focus solely on what you can control. Let everything else go. You will be amazed at how different you will feel after reflecting on how much thought you place on things you have no control over. Once you stop worrying about things outside of your control you will unlock unbelievable potential previously unexplored.

Physical AMRAP – 8 minutes:

Set a clock for eight minutes and perform as many rounds as possible of ten push-ups and twenty air squats.

To perform the air squat, start standing with your feet at about your shoulder's width apart, heels down, and feet slightly turned out. First, send your hips back almost as if you were sitting into a chair while simultaneously bending your knees. Continue to sit until the crease of your hip is below the top of your knee or "below parallel." Once to proper depth, stand back to full extension by pressing through your heels and extending your legs.

Jason's Pro-Tip: Remember, if you need assistance in the push-up you can perform this exercise from your knees. In the air squat, if you are unable to squat to the depth described above without discomfort you should only go as low as you are able. As you get more accustomed to the squat, your body will adapt to this new range of motion.

CHAPTER 4

THE ONLY REAL-LIFE HACK…WORK REALLY HARD

R emember those airport bookstores and the ridiculous books that line the shelves? There's a thriving business not only in selling books with no substance, but also those that promise you the ability to hack your way to wealth or health. Lounging around won't make you millions, and it won't get you great abs! I wish that were true, but it just isn't the case. Now there are certainly tips, tools, and tricks to mastering certain skills or accomplishing goals, but anything worthwhile will surely only come through hard work and dedication. For me, it's less about the amount of time something may take and more about the effort—can you go from couch slouch to hard body in a few short months? Sure can. But you better believe you'll have to change everything about your life and work harder than you ever imagined.

Another way to describe this breed of no-effort life hacking is *taking the easy way out*. It's my opinion that millennials have especially been caught up in the "hack your way to _____" craze. I have one burning question, and I bet you guessed it based on the title of this chapter: what's wrong with good ol', roll-up-your-sleeves hard work? Just about everyone I know who has achieved anything of value had to work hard to do it. When people ask me what my secret is, I'm always a little embarrassed by how simple it sounds. I often respond with, "It's not a secret at all…I just worked really hard for many, many years."

I think it's a little unfortunate that we live in a time when hacking one's way to success is an alluring market of its own. Isn't it common knowledge that hidden within every shortcut is a cost? At some point you *will* have to pay. Even if by some stroke of luck you are able to "hack" your way to a goal, have you really mastered the skills that you needed to master? Have you built, brick by brick, the foundation of confidence you'll rely on in the future? Will you be able to replicate your results in the future? Or did you just play yourself?

YOU CAN'T "HACK" YOUR WAY AROUND HARD WORK

When I was young, I was fortunate to learn a few foundational principals from mentors. Show up on a consistent basis every day for weeks, months, and years on end. When you show up, you show up on time, ready to work, and you work…hard. These are non-negotiable. You show up. You're on time. You work. And you work hard. *Honestly* hard.

Because I experienced some success in competitive CrossFit I tend to get more than a few messages daily from people who are not currently training but want to win the CrossFit Games…this year. Not in five years, not in two years, heck…not even next year. *This* year. For those who wake up one day and decide they want to win the CrossFit Games, they first have to undergo a reality check and understand what they're up against.

You're talking about a competition that literally begins by pitting you against the world, and then ends with you up against the world's best. The competition just to get to the Games (let alone be in a position to win it) is as large as it is fierce. Your level of fitness and the resolve of your why is going to have to have an otherworldly strength. The race to be good enough to have a shot at even qualifying for the Games has made training a full-time job…for years. And that's just the physical element. If you qualify, competing at the Games requires a much-sharpened set of emotional and psychological tools.

Bottom line: there's no hacking your way to the top of anything. It's certainly not possible in professional sports. The same can be said for building a robust, successful business, and for building a long-term, happy relationship. The price of entry is a long grind packed with challenges, and the sooner you recognize that, the sooner you will be able to use the AMRAP Mentality to its greatest potential. It has to be something you love doing, want very badly, and want for the right reasons.

My definition of hard work is probably best characterized by the level of intensity you give to the work at hand. This ties back to the topic of the previous chapter: focus. When you need to accomplish a task, block out all distractions and get to work. Your ability to work hard scales with your ability to focus. To elevate your performance in pursuing your best work, make an AMRAP-style workout of it. Compete against yourself on a clock and try to do a better job today than you did yesterday. Or (and only if you're ready…) if you really want to punch the throttle, compete against others.

This is the same concept that makes community-based fitness so successful. When you shut off the noise, commit to the grind, and add a touch of competitive energy, you are going to see the results. The process pays double. Not only will you see immediate improvement in your current output, but also you will get better at the process each time you show up, punch the clock, and put in the work. Improvement occurs naturally through consistent practice. The combination of consistent practice and competition will set your results on fire. Ever pour a little lighter fluid into an open flame? I just gave you a can of lighter fluid...now, use it.

Hard Work + Consistency = Results

Of course, this conversation about hard work doesn't occur in vacuum. It depends on you—where are you are now, where are you coming from, and where are you going? Working hard doesn't mean that you're pushing yourself into a reckless, potentially dangerous downward spiral. It doesn't mean you go shooting off in some random direction. Rather, it means pushing past your comfort zone and systematically testing your limits.

Let's compare the concept to exercise. The workout necessary to produce the desired result necessarily will involve a relative level of discomfort. The key word is *relative*. The level of input is going to be much different for an inactive person on their first day at the gym than for a seasoned, well-trained athlete. However, they both need to work hard relative to their physical, psychological, and emotional capacities. One of the things we do at NCFIT is provide an experience that shows new clients what hard work in a gym looks like while keeping them safe. We toss them in the deep end, but with a stellar set of floaties and with a vigilant lifeguard on duty.

In this context, I like to use the term "best effort" (or even "smartest effort") and often avoid the term "max effort." There's a subtle difference. *Make your best effort* clearly denotes that I am asking for hard work, but not hard work at the expense of safety. You might ask, "But Jason, how would you know I am truly giving my best effort?" Honestly...*I* won't. Only you can. I could certainly make a guess, based on previous observations and experience.

However, you are the only one who knows whether you make your best effort or whether you fake your way through it. The onus is on you. I can give you the tools, but I can't do the work for you. So, if you're okay with mediocrity and just getting by…go ahead, fake it.

But here's the promise: if you truly work hard, if you truly show up every damn day and make your best effort…you'll achieve results. This is going to happen in the gym, at work, and in life. Forget the hacks and shortcuts. Practicing, and eventually mastering, hard work is the only sure path towards reaching your true potential.

THE VALUE OF STRONG MENTORS

Let me tell you about three of the hardest workers I've ever met, and the lessons I learned from them. I met two of them while learning the ropes of the gym business from behind a desk—Joe and Minh. Through their actions and invaluable counsel, I learned a great deal about what to do and how to do it…for just about anything life can throw at you. And through their stories I learned about common pitfalls and what *not* to do. Later, I put these lessons to use when I went into business for myself.

Joe owned the gym. He is a barrel-chested bear of man with no off switch. I spent a lot of time watching, shadowing, quizzing, and following him. I fired questions at him constantly. *A lot of questions*. Questions about the basic operations of a fitness business, how to lease a space, identifying prime locations, dealing with members, managing staff, and turning a profit.

I truly think Joe saw how much I was burning to be successful, and for the most part, he was happy to offer advice. I was disciplined and hardworking, and I knew Joe valued that more than anything. He knew that I studied my craft and practiced my sales pitch. He could see that I sincerely wanted to help people make health and fitness part of their lifestyles. We both shared the belief that fitness could change lives.

By the time I started working for Joe, he'd gone from selling memberships to buying and selling properties. He had built a highly successful fitness business with multiple locations in the San Jose area. He knew entrepreneurship, and I unrelentingly peppered him with questions about how to do it. I thought that if Joe knew it, I should know it too.

In fact, Joe taught me one of the most powerful lessons of my life. He probably doesn't even remember the talk, but I sure do. One night as we powered along on the elliptical, I worked up the courage to tell Joe that one day I wanted to own a gym. I was nervous as hell…I remember trying to sound really cool and prepared. It went something like this…

"Joe, I want to own a gym one day."

Yep, that's it. It was all I could muster. But I'll never forget what he said in reply.

"If you want to be an owner, Jason, then act like an owner."

Without another word, he hopped off the elliptical and walked away. This left me feeling a little confused, and I wasn't entirely sure how to interpret the quick departure. About thirty minutes later, I saw Joe again. This time he was on his hands and knees cleaning a mess that someone had made in the bathroom. It hit me right across the face. If I wanted to be an owner, manager, or the like, I needed to start acting like it. Not then but now. Not tomorrow but today. From that day on, I cleaned the bathrooms nearly every day and picked up every piece of garbage I saw on the floor. I even started to wear a collared shirt, and if you know me, this is a BIG DEAL. To this day, I won't walk by trash on the floor. And every time I visit one of our gyms, my first stop is the bathroom…to ensure they are up to the standards I learned from Joe.

My education from Minh revolved around the art of the sale.

He was an absolute master. You might recall that I didn't start off as a sales guy at Joe's gym. At first, I worked the front desk and made $12 an hour. From my desk-height metal stool, I would watch Minh with awe. My eyes followed him as he greeted perspective new members at the door and ushered them quickly into his office. Minh knew I was watching him. He loved it. He occasionally made sure that I saw his commission checks as the came across the front desk. If he was trying to inspire me to move up to sales, it worked.

Minh was the gym's best sales guy by a wide margin. A perennial top-performer, Minh could sell a ketchup Popsicle to a man in white gloves. He had perfected the art of the sale, and he had done so after working up from nothing.

Minh was born in Vietnam, and once he and his family moved to the United States, they moved around a lot—Texas, Florida, and finally California. When Minh started school, he didn't know any English, but he worked his way through it and graduated high school.

By the time he was eighteen, Minh was considering college but there was no family money to send him. They simply couldn't afford it. So instead, he worked. It started simply, with a help wanted ad. He took down the address and showed up. When Minh arrived, he received two things: a box and instructions. The box was filled with women's perfumes. And the instructions were simple… sell them. As you might imagine, the first day wasn't much fun. Minh didn't know anything about perfume. And the first time he knocked on a door, he was scared to death. It was not comfortable at all. He would freeze up the instant someone answered, then turn away without a word and head toward the next house. He felt the urge to quit and be done with it. But he didn't quit. He learned to embrace the discomfort and worked his way through it.

Like Joe, I think Minh saw something in me. That's why he made sure I saw his commission checks. Later he would tell me that he noticed my hustle. Minh's work ethic was guided by the singular maxim—*if you can sell, you can eat.*

Eventually, Minh took me under his wing. From him, I learned the basics of selling technique and the importance of resilience. My skills improved quickly. A big part of this was the energy and enthusiasm I showed potential customers. Minh approved and sought to magnify this trait in me. He helped me shape a personal policy of how to treat people, a policy I honor to this day.

Later in my career, I reflected on my performances and realized I needed some help. Chris, the last mentor I want to talk about, was a member of NCFIT, and had extensive experience in triathlons. It was definitely an area I needed a lot of help in!

I looked at my results from the Games events, where I placed top ten in almost everything. The outliers were the endurance events, in which I was at the bottom of the pack. I knew I needed to work on my weaknesses if I wanted to get back on the podium. I met Chris in 2012, and he completely changed my game.

In 2011, they announced a triathlon at Camp Pendleton. I didn't sleep all night because I was so nervous, and Ashley played a large part in calming me down.

Fast forward two years later, and I walked into both 2013 and some long endurance events with the earned confidence to do well. All the track workouts, swimming, and biking had paid off. Learning how to compete had certainly paid off.

One thing Chris taught me was to "break the rubber band." I use this analogy in business to this day.

Let's say runners are in a pack, and two of them break away from the group and are neck and neck. All of a sudden, the second group realizes there's no way to catch those two and they start fighting for third place. The leaders of the race have slipped their minds.

The goal is to break the rubber band between the runner leading in first and the person coming in second. If two runners are within a few feet of each other, it can help the second runner to imagine a band drawn between the two. That band is what will keep the second runner mentally and physically in the game. Once the gap between the two runners becomes twenty feet or so, the runner in second place is no longer looking to compete with the runner in first. In other words, the band has broken and the second place competitor has shifted his or her mindset. Now, he or she is trying to maintain second, and is running to avoid being overtaken by those competing for third.

This mentality can be seen in business as well. Establish yourself as such a powerful leader that your "competitors" are no longer striving to catch up to you, but instead are working "outrun" the men or women competing for their title or role. Once you've done this, you've broken the band.

In a way, this is the essence of the AMRAP Mentality. The goal is not to work as long as possible before dropping of exhaustion, the goal is to work as smartly as possible in order to make the most of the time you have. Think of it as a results-driven system rather than a time-driven one.

I learned a great deal from my mentors. Don't work to the detriment of your family. Use your time wisely. Don't judge anyone. Treat everyone with respect. Greet all newcomers with a friendly smile and encouraging energy. Use well-placed humor to break down barriers. Let the client know you are there for them. Allow your client space and time to make their decision.

What this all boils down to is being friendly, treating the client with respect, and allowing them to feel comfortable in an environment I knew could be intimidating. A smile and positive energy were the best ways to do this.

Minh taught me that selling requires real passion. If you've ever met me, you know that if I am anything it's fired up! I genuinely enjoy talking to people about fitness. I always have, and I always will. This made the sell something more genuine. I was actually really excited about helping these new clients get started. My sales strategy, if that's what you'd call it, was simple: smile and listen. When I discovered what it was that had motivated them to come into the gym, their why, I focused on that. I let them know how the gym could help, and I explained to them the value of a fit, healthy life.

If a prospective client didn't buy a membership that day, it wasn't a problem. I never showed any frustration or belittled their decision. I simply let them know that they could call me anytime, and I would be there if they changed their mind. Not only was this the right thing to do, but also it was good business. Funny how often those two line up! Many of the same folks who had walked out without buying a membership came back two months, six months, a year later or sometimes longer. This approach paid dividends, as people would specifically ask for me and tell their friends and coworkers about me. I was feeling pretty stoked. In a few short years, I went from front desk towel boy to Minh's closest "rival" on the sales board.

I was making very good money and feeling pretty good about myself. I gained more momentum and began to focus my entire schedule and lifestyle on optimizing my sales output. I went to classes in the morning, went to the gym in the afternoon, and sold memberships until the gym closed for the night. Looking back on it, I was definitely using the AMRAP Mentality already, I just didn't know it. All the pieces were there…I was segmenting my day into clear time slots, identifying a clear focus for each endeavor, and attacking each with purpose. But most importantly, I had a burning passion within me. I was fighting for a comfortable life with Ashley, and I was beginning to get a taste of being my own boss.

At this point in my life, making money really fired me up. I could travel with Ashley and take her out for nice dinners. Our relationship continued to grow, and I was already saving for a ring. I gained more and more freedom, and I didn't cause my parents any additional stress by asking for money. It was a good situation. However, and still to this day, I will not let money define me. Money is a means to an end. But money is also unforgiving and if you're not careful, it will consume you.

To this day, I keep in contact with Joe and Minh. Not much has changed for them. Joe still runs a thriving business in San Jose. And Minh, well…maybe a lot changed for Minh. Minh is no longer selling gym memberships. He's actually not selling *anything* anymore, which is weird to think about! Minh retired young, and he is enjoying life.

YOUR WHY IS YOUR ANCHOR

Anything worth achieving is going to take some real effort. At times, you'll be cruising and all will be well in the world. But other times, it will feel like the world is closing in on you, and you want to do anything but continue forward. *Oh @#*!*. A strong why for each of the focuses you choose is especially necessary in these dark times. Your why will help you bounce back from hard times, bad days, and defeat. It will jump-start you. And if it's strong enough it may even start to make you *enjoy* the hard times for the potential growth they offer.

In July 2009, I experienced another significant test of my resolve. At the time, I was the reigning CrossFit Games champ. It happened in the middle of the first event of the 2009 CrossFit Games, and I found myself faced with a choice.

I was five miles into a seven-mile off-road run. I felt like I was dying. I had my headphones turned up as loud as they could go, desperate to drown out the sound of my own breathing. The run had actually become more like a crawl…I was on all fours, grasping at clumps of earth for a good part of the race. As a side note, I also managed to get poison oak from this same hill run, which made getting married soon after the Games interesting!

Of course, I had run this distance before. I had done it in worse conditions too. But this time, the intensity blocked out any training I had done. With everything on the line, my body started to shut down. The intense stress, the loud music in my ears, and the desire to win (or die trying) all compounded. As I neared the last portion of the run, I collapsed. In an instant I was on the ground, passed out, and barely breathing.

It so happens that this all went down right in front of my family, friends, and dozens of NorCal CrossFit members. I can't imagine how Ashley felt at that moment. The guy she was going to marry had just fallen flat on his back. And he wasn't moving.

I remember slowly coming back to reality. Dave Castro, director of the CrossFit Games, hunched over me and asked, "Jason, do you want to continue? If not, your CrossFit Games are over." It took me a minute to realize what was happening, but once the fog wore off, I managed to reply, "Absolutely, I will continue." I slowly stood up and stumbled to the side, where I grabbed a random spectator's water bottle. (Sorry, random fan! I know that must have been kind of gross, but it didn't matter at the time.) For the next few hundred meters all I thought about was the next step. Each step was meaningful, each step a battle unto itself. There was no thinking, no feeling bad for myself…it simply was *GO*. I finished the event.

Even though I managed to finish, I did so at the bottom of the pack. For the next few events, I had to claw and fight for every point, just like I had clawed and fought up that hill. When it was all said and done I had gone from nearly last to fifth place overall. That year, I was awarded the Spirit of the Games honors, an annual award given to the athlete that best exemplifies the work, camaraderie, and perseverance to which CrossFit aspires.

I continued the event not because of the prize money or to get more followers on social media. My decision came from a deep, burning drive to follow through on the commitments I had made to myself. I was honoring my why. All of the sacrifices, all of the training, all of the sleepless nights had helped prepare me for that one moment. It was a test. I don't think anyone would have judged me if I had chosen not to continue. But *I* wouldn't have been able to live with myself. I've replayed that moment over and over again, thousands of times in my head. I use Dave's words often in my self-talk: *Jason, do you want to continue?*

ABSOLUTELY, I WILL CONTINUE

The Games were a cumulative test of my commitment to see what my body was truly capable of, to challenge myself against the best, and to ultimately trade high levels of discomfort for growth. My why in competition had become transcending my past results and pushing my body's limits. I wanted to do more. Fitness has always been a top priority in my life. Ever since I was young, I have enjoyed training to improve the way I look and feel. In my early teens, I used to compete in BMX. To prepare for races I would ride my bike on rollers in my garage while listening to Blink 182's *Enema of the State* on repeat. I realized early on that it was my responsibility to put in the work, and how I finished in the race reflected my level of commitment.

My love for fitness reached new heights when I started competing in the CrossFit Games. Competing in the Games was an amazing adventure for nearly ten years of my life. I was privileged to compete as an individual seven times and once as part of a team. Each year, I would evaluate whether I was ready to make the commitment to compete again the following year. During my tenure stepping on to the floor, my answer was always *absolutely*. I was highly motivated to win, and I wanted to prove to myself that I could compete with the best.

If you're not powered by wanting something with all your heart and soul, it will be easy to give in when things get uncomfortable. Think of a few tough workouts you have had (or boardroom meetings). Did you power through the discomfort as best you could? Or did you slouch over, grip your shorts (or slacks), look around at the people nearby, take a sip of water, and only *then* get back to your work? I've been there. What I want to tell you is that the strong desire you need to employ in reaching your fitness goals is the same for business, relationships, and life. You can't just stop when it gets hard.

The only thing that can turn your motivation into meaningful progress is hard work. You may be committed to overcoming adverse conditions, and you may desire reaching a goal more than anything else in the world. In short, you might have a fierce and powerful and meaningful why. But desire is not enough. Motivation is not enough. Knowledge is not enough, and mentors are not enough.

You need all these things, but the only way they can make change in your life is by gritting your teeth and putting in the work.

I know I talk a lot about bicycles, but bear with me one more time. You might have the fanciest, fastest bike in the world. You might have a killer plan for how you are going to hit a thirty-mile target. You might have all the gear you need, you might have fine-tuned your diet and talked to the greatest coaches in the world. But none of those things, as awesome as they are, make the pedals turn. The only thing that can do that—is your hard work.

How well you perform under adverse conditions is a good indicator of how in-tune you are with your purpose (and whether you've identified your true purpose in the first place). If things all of the sudden get hard and you lose interest in suffering through... you honestly don't want it badly enough. You need to reassess. Whether or not you're aligned with the right purpose is a good place to start when doing a postmortem analysis of a failure. If you're consistently failing, you need to evaluate your why and what you are choosing to focus on. Sometimes, we need help in battling through discomfort—that's okay. To take action in realizing your why, find a good mentor, coach, or group of friends to help you figure out the best path.

READER EXERCISE

Mindfulness AMRAP – 15 Minutes:

Set a clock for fifteen minutes and write down five or six hardworking people in your circle of influence that share similar desires for self-improvement and collaboration. Next, narrow the list down to two or three people that because of mindset, relationship, or proximity might be interested in forming a small group centered on sharing experiences and new ideas. Draft an email gauging their interest in getting together this week or next to talk about living, working, or training to the fullest potential. Propose a date, time, and location. It may turn out to be a one-time occurrence but valuable nonetheless. However, if you foster healthy, inclusive, and positive conversation, it is more than likely you will find the group willing to meet again.

Physical AMRAP – 12 Minutes:

Grab a partner and set a clock for twelve minutes. While you are working, your partner will be holding a plank position. You will complete a full round, then switch with your partner, allowing them to complete a full round. Continue this rotation for all twelve minutes. Each round will consist of ten step-ups, twelve sit-ups, and fourteen jumping jacks.

To perform the step-up, first find a sturdy object like a box, bench, or stoop. Stand squarely in front of the object and step up and step down with the same leg. Alternate legs each time you step up onto the object. Every time you step up, that is one repetition.

To perform the sit-up, start seated on the ground with your legs in a comfortable position (straight, crossed, or knees bent). Sit back under control until your shoulders touch the ground, then immediately sit up so that your torso finishes perpendicular to the ground. Each time you sit up, that is one repetition.

To perform the jumping jack, start standing with your feet and arms extended. Jump and bring your hands and feet together at the same time. Each time you clap, that is one repetition.

Jason's Pro-Tip: Partner workouts are a lot of fun! Don't worry so much about the score on this one, but rather focus on communicating with your partner and having a good time. Make sure you play some really good tunes and end the workout with a few crisp high-fives!

CHAPTER 5

THE ART OF SHIFTING GEARS

Part of the AMRAP Mentality that I spent extensive and deliberate time developing (and still do today) is the concept of switching focuses throughout the day. It was first sparked on the day I was walking with Ava and Ashley in 2011, and over the next few years it came into even sharper focus. It is no exaggeration to say that learning to shift gears is the real key to the Mentality, especially in my case. Hard work came naturally to me since I had so many great role models in my formative years. But staying focused on the right thing at the right time did not.

For anyone who has important goals in different areas of life—education, career, family, finance, spirit—it can be difficult to prioritize and focus. It's hard not getting overwhelmed by it all. It's very common that when you start excelling in one area that other areas start to suffer. Like anyone else, I wrestled with this issue. As my family grew larger when Ava was born, our business started to grow globally, and the CrossFit Games became more challenging, it became more important than ever to segment my day.

In 2010, the CrossFit Games were held for the first time at the StubHub Center in Carson, California. This was big time for the

CrossFit community. Reebok and CrossFit had just signed a major deal that would make Reebok the title sponsor of the Games. The prizes quadrupled from the previous year, and we weren't throwing down out at a ranch out in the middle of nowhere anymore—in every sense, we had arrived as professional athletes for a legit sport. So, there was much more on the line. Having placed first in 2008 and fifth in 2009, I felt like I was one of the favorites to win.

I was confident that my preparation through 2009 and 2010 was dialed in. I thought I was in the best shape of my life. But when I got to Carson, something suddenly didn't feel right. I remember being constantly anxious, completely unable to control my nerves. At the time I didn't know it, but I think *perceived* versus *earned* confidence played a big role here.

I sure thought I had trained hard, but had I really? Was I really as prepared as my peers? We would soon find out.

I was in the last heat of the night. We found ourselves under the lights, with ESPN cameras following our every move. Right before the heat started, the national anthem played and jets flew over the stadium. The stadium erupted. I was fired up!

Maybe a little too fired up. After leading the entire event and with only ten reps to finish, my body began to shut down. It felt like 2009 all over again. I'm not sure if it was the anxiety, the capacity crowd, going too hard and too fast, or a combination of all of that, but I ended up on the floor for an hour after the event. I could barely move. They finally carted me off when it was clear I wasn't going anywhere on my own. A few hours later, I had to be lifted into the car. I vaguely remember going to a restaurant well after the event, still in a daze.

What followed was a deep psychological setback. For all intents and purposes, I was out of it—mentally and physically. There was a lot more competition coming in the next couple of days, and

I knew that I had to get my mind right. I made a commitment to step up and complete the Games with a promise that I would spend time afterwards evaluating what had happened, and why.

I kept my promise, and though I finished my worst career Games by placement (sixteenth), I did finish. When I had recovered, I began to evaluate my performance. It didn't take time to realize that something was off, and that I knew exactly what it was.

I was married, with the clear intent to build a family. My business was thriving, and I had begun to pour even more energy into that career. The issue, I understood over time, was that I hadn't compartmentalized my day well. I wasn't putting in the training focus that was required to compete at the highest level. I was stretching myself too thin, and unintelligently. I remember taking business calls and trying to train right before or after, and it wasn't working well.

This, in conjunction with worrying about factors outside my control, were two immediate and major areas I could improve on. For the next four years, I would compete and perform very well, and I attribute most of this to recognizing the importance of switching gears and remaining focused on the task at hand.

THE ESSENCE OF THE SHIFT

I knew the area I wanted to focus on, but just knowing isn't enough; you need to analyze, prioritize, and execute. It is challenging to work concurrently toward multiple desired end states without effectively shifting gears between them. Thinking about one when you are working on another is a recipe for disaster. Switching gears provides the mental and physical adjustment necessary to align your focus to the proper task.

Let me take you through a typical morning. I start each day at

5 a.m.—*first gear*. At this hour, my wife and kids are still sleeping. This is my time to focus on fitness.

A few years back, I converted my garage into a home gym. You might think a guy who runs an international fitness business might go all out for his personal gym, but that's not the case. My space is very simple. Some iron, a few barbells, a pullup bar…that's all I need for go time.

I slowly rev up my body and start to get after it. During this time, I am thinking of nothing but the task in front of me. I don't answer emails, take calls, or have the TV on. My focus is singular and clear: for thirty minutes to an hour, I work as hard as I can. I leave everything on the floor, every workout. I don't have a "just cruise" pace. Despite all the other noise in my life, this is my time to free my mind and test my body. By the end of my workout, I am ready to take on the rest of my day.

At around 6 a.m., I walk back in the house and turn on dad-mode—*second gear*. Going to the office and visiting our NCFIT gyms for a class will occur later in the day.

Family time is sacred time. Once my wife and kids wake for the day, I am fully invested in them. I don't think about my workout and what I could've done better, faster, or heavier—it's irrelevant and out of my mind. Any worrying about fitness at this point would be a waste of my precious time with family. This is really the essence of shifting gears. When you're in the moment…be in the moment. Being present is not only one of the greatest tools we have to ensure productivity and focus, but also one of life's greatest rewards. You will find fulfillment and meaning in even the smallest tasks. You will learn to appreciate life in the moment and slowly stop living in the future or past.

A common characteristic of people who find themselves unhappy, unfulfilled, or unsuccessful is an inability to live in the moment. Often people will beat themselves up about the past (the good ol' days or what they *could've* done) or incessantly think about the future (how good things will be *only when*…). Fatally flawed. What these people don't realize is that this type of mindset precludes any chance of happiness. The next few words are bold but true. It will be challenging, if not impossible, to find true happiness if you can't stop living in the past or worrying about the future. Having goals (which live in the future) and learning from your mistakes (which reside in the past) is completely different and undeniably beneficial. However, if you find yourself in the position where your thoughts are consumed by what was or what could be…you need to snap out of it, and fast.

HOPE FOR THE BEST, PREPARE FOR THE WORST

As I mentioned earlier in this book, my father had a version of leukemia when I was young. I was around fourteen years old at the time. He hid it from us very well, to keep from causing extra anxiety at home; he travelled a lot for work and would make it seem like he was travelling when in reality he was in the hospital. He eventually found out about an experimental drug and sought out treatment with it. It worked, and within a few years my father was cancer-free. I bring this up because of events that would take place many years later, at a time when I learned a tough lesson about perspective.

Fast forward to a few weeks after Ava's diagnosis. At this point, it had really kicked in what we were up against. Ava had her first bone marrow sample taken, and it was sent away for analysis for two days. When it came back, Ashley and I went through one of the more traumatizing moments of our time in the hospital.

After bone marrow analysis, cancer treatment centers put together a sort of profile for patients and their families, charting out treatment plans and schedules, things to be expected, and what could go wrong. When the time came, Ashley, my father, and I were called into a room, where we were presented with a thick, three-ring binder that contained Ava's profile. The atmosphere was so heavy...the seriousness was palpable.

The doctor began taking us through the profile. For these things, you are really presented with all the worst-case scenarios. Ava would lose all her hair. She wouldn't be able to go to school. She would have to wear a mask at all times to protect her weakened immune system. And on and on and on. The thought of what our little girl might have to go through was overwhelming, and I found myself hardening from the inside out. I steeled myself against what might happen in the future, because it was only at my strongest that I would be able to beat this thing with Ava.

Now, my dad is a level-headed and smart guy, and he had been through this exact experience when he had battled cancer. At one point in the meeting, he turned to me and said, "Jason, trust me; it won't be as bad as they just said."

This was not what I needed to hear at that point. I didn't want hope, or coddling, or the promise of an easier time. I responded, "Dad, with all due respect, I hope you are right, but right now, I *need* to expect the worst. This is the information they have given me, and this is the information I have to work with."

Of course, my dad was right. It didn't end up as bad as the doctor had said, even though some things did happen. She did have to wear a mask for a long time, and she was put under general anesthesia twenty-seven times.

By giving us the worst-case scenario, they were just trying to get across to us the reality of what we were up against. Ashley and I needed to understand the severity of the situation in order to do what needed to be done, and any slack on our part would have been a liability if it had ended up being much worse.

When it comes to the AMRAP Mentality, it can be beneficial to expect the worst, and anticipate the ways things might go wrong. Why wouldn't you prepare for unplanned events, if you could? Of course, there is a fine line between expecting the worst with the proper attitude, and expecting the worst and getting bogged down by anxiety and fear. In this sea, your guiding star will always be your why; keep it in sight, and you will be able to accomplish what you need to accomplish.

SHIFTING TO THE RIGHT PERSPECTIVE

Staying present and shifting gears also allows you to maintain proper perspective. I relied on this heavily when Ava got sick. The long stints in the hospital were physically and emotionally draining. Ava counted on us to be upbeat and positive, and everything about the situation was fighting against my ability to be so. I knew I had to employ the gear shift to keep me as energized as possible during my time by Ava's side.

A critical element of this, for me, is working out. Fitness brings me life, energy, and vigor. If I had those things, I knew I could bring positive energy to her hospital room. In order to keep my activities segmented, I worked out extremely early, extremely late, or during times when Ava would sleep or had to undergo a long procedure (and then, only if we couldn't be by her side the entire time). I worked out anywhere I could find space—the parking lot, quiet room, up and down the hospital stairs. Once my workout was complete, I immediately switched gears to return to my family or check in on my daughter.

The switch is sharp and immediate. When I was first refining this technique, I would often remind myself, firmly and out loud, that a shift has occurred. *Jason, stay focused!* This simple exclamation would shock me back into the moment (I'm sure it also shocked anyone in earshot!). I continue this practice to this day. Now that Ava is on the road to recovery, my days are hectic in a much different way. Most days, my calendar is packed, front to back, with updates, meetings, and calls. I'm usually in business-mode—*third gear*. If I'm not careful, I can get distracted or thrown off by thinking about what just went down or what's coming next.

What's worked for me is generally keeping appointments on my calendar to one hour or less. When the task or meeting finishes, I take a quick inventory of the past hour, then immediately shift forward. Generally, I like to review on an hour-by-hour basis, as many times as possible throughout the day. Even just for a deep breath to organize my thoughts. If you were walking around our office or one of our gyms, there's still a good chance you might hear me remind myself—*Jason, stay focused!*

THE GOTTA GO PLAN

If you and I were throwing down together in a workout, you might hear me say, "GOTTA GO!" In fact, when training for the CrossFit Games, I would say this so often that my training partners started talking about the Gotta Go Plan. Essentially, "gotta go" meant we had to hustle harder, whether between movements in a workout or between workouts in a series. To get the most out of our training, or to get the fastest time on the workout, we needed to *hustle*. If we were slow in our transitions, time would hemorrhage off the clock and we would be behind the eight ball. Not because we weren't fit enough…just because we were being lazy. Similarly, if we wasted too much time messing around in the gym when we should have been working out, we lost precious time later in the day. Much of my success in fitness can be attributed to two simple things—first, I trained as hard as I wanted to win; second, I hustled through parts of workouts or transitions where other people might take as a rest. The AMRAP Mentality and the Gotta Go Plan complement one another beautifully.

FITNESS, FAMILY, BUSINESS, AND THE ART OF THE SHIFT

Just like having focus without hard work is a recipe for failure, working hard without switching gears is, too. A large piece of switching gears is keeping your mind and body focused and present. By shifting between different focuses, you can stay fresh and perform to the best of your ability. It is critical to maintain the work ethic mentioned above through each focus.

A shift in gears could be as simple as a rural farmer taking off early to get something done on the property, returning home to enjoy a meal together with his family, and repeating the process the next day. The farmer in this scenario might not shift gears too many times each day, but just this simple back and forth between responsibilities is a clear example of shifting gears. Or this could be as complex as a single parent with a leadership job having to prioritize and reprioritize meetings, appointments, and deadlines with the always shifting demands of making sure his or her kids get to and from day care, to doctor's appointments, to say nothing of quality time at home! In this scenario, there might be many more gears needed and shifting will happen multiple times a day.

Regardless of the situation, we all need to segment our day to accommodate our goals. My understanding of this principle took time to develop. There was a time when I couldn't sit down to dinner with my family without my thoughts being swept off to business matters or training problems. I was doing a poor job of switching gears and staying focused in the moment. I now challenge myself daily to chop up my day into different gears, prioritize what those gears need to be for the day, and stay focused on each one while I am in it.

The AMRAP Mentality borrows so much from fitness. In fact, the best way I've found to practice the AMRAP Mentality *outside of the gym* is by perfecting the AMRAP Mentality *inside the gym.* During AMRAP-style training, you have a set amount of time to get as much work done as possible. If the goal of the workout is to be as productive as possible, you will need a keen understanding of your capacity, goals (short term in the workout, and long term in *all* your training), previous performances, current training state, current conditions, ideal pace for besting your goal, areas in the workout you can push harder, and areas in the workout you need to show restraint. In life, the only thing that's different is the task at hand. Literally everything else is the same…so why would you approach the rest of your life any differently than a properly-tackled workout?

Think of this parallel. You find yourself five minutes into a thirty-minute workout, and the world is closing in on you. You came out too hot, misjudged your abilities, made a mistake in movement, reps, or loading…for whatever reason, you're sinking fast. You have the ability to change the outcome. Simply swallow your pride and make whatever adjustments need to be made and use what you have learned from the mentality to stabilize.

On the flip side of the same scenario, five minutes into a thirty-minute workout, you are absolutely crushing it! You're on your pace, feeling like a million bucks, and clearly seeing your goal come to life. Brilliant! In this case, the AMRAP Mentality can help you keep riding that high and stay on pace to meet your goal. Look at the clock, understand the time elapsed / remaining, and try to hold a similar pace for the time remaining.

All the while, evaluate. This real-time feedback will help you perform your best during your workouts. Now, taken into the real world for pursuits in life or business, this practice is a great way to ensure success. Often, it's only after a workout (or life event) that we reflect on how we did. Certainly, post-mortem analysis is undeniably valuable and necessary; however, if you were able to change a tactic, technique, or tempo in the moment in a way that would help ensure a successful outcome…why wouldn't you? This isn't always easy, and sometimes it's hard to see the forest for the trees when you're in the thick of it. This gets easier with time and training. The more you practice and the more you put yourself in the moment, the better you will be at achieving your desired results in the amount of time you set.

Life outside the gym offers endless opportunities to employ the gear shift. When properly applied, you can get a lot done in a finite amount of time, all the while staying present and invested. A simple way to bring this to life right now is by using the timer on your watch or phone. Next time you're washing the dishes, doing yard work, or reviewing work documents, set your watch for a certain amount of time and go. See how you perform with this tiny hint of pressure to get a maximum amount of quality work done in a set amount of time. (Just make sure you don't break any dishes because you are going too fast!)

Does the timing aspect make it more fun, or to use the term in fashion these days, *gamify* it for you? Do you start to sweat or get anxious even knowing there's a clock on you? Do you get way more done than you expected, or did you spend most of the time scrolling through Instagram? The answers to these questions are all valuable feedback. Once the time is up, quickly evaluate your work, and switch gears to the next task. By using the techniques of the AMRAP Mentality, you'll be keeping your mind in check. Your thoughts won't drift so easily, and you won't get distracted from the work you need—and want—to get done. My biggest fear is that I will wake up ten years from now only to regret the decisions I made, or long for the time I wasted. Staying present, evaluating my performance in real time, and shifting gears is my hedge against this potential outcome.

READER EXERCISE

Mindfulness AMRAP – 10 Minutes:

Set a clock for ten minutes and plan your upcoming day on a blank piece of paper. Be prepared to plan the time you wake, until the time you turn in.

This will involve some forward thinking about your assignments, meals, family time, and training. Keep blocks of time to within thirty minutes to two hours unless it is absolutely necessary to book longer. Even if you need to block eight hours for work, add five-to ten-minute breaks to keep you fresh.

During each block, your goal is to give 100% of your time and attention to the current endeavor. Try to hold yourself accountable to the plan. Before the end of the day, review your schedule in comparison to your execution. If you notice room for improvement in time management or focus, write it down and make short notes about what happened.

Physical AMRAP – 10 Minutes:

Set a clock for ten minutes and perform as many rounds as possible of 200m run, followed by thirty seconds of walking rest. No matter where you are in the workout (running or rest) at the top of each minute, perform five burpees. At the start of the workout, perform five burpees then immediately start your run. Once one minute elapses, stop and perform five more burpees. Continue until you reach ten minutes.

Jason's Pro-Tip: You will need to have a watch handy for this one, so make sure you plan ahead. Minding the clock is an essential part of the AMRAP Mentality. Know where you are in your workout, your work, your day at all times. Make sure you don't miss any of those burpees!

CHAPTER 6

MOMENTS OF RE-EVALUATION

The final stage of the AMRAP Mentality, re-evaluation, is a high-level review of yourself, designed to ensure you stay oriented towards true north. As time passes, life changes, and goals are either realized or not. Your core motivations and true north, your *why*, may shift, change, or adjust. This is normal as life progresses and situations change. Timely re-evaluations keep you focused on what really matters and cut away the things that don't.

These sweeping re-evaluations do not need to occur daily or weekly; instead, they should be performed when life changes dramatically or when you do or don't achieve a long-term goal. I like to call these major instances *moments*. These are moments in time when it seems like the universe is conspiring to tell you something. Whether that something is to keep charging ahead, change directions, subtly adjust, or stop in your tracks will depend on the time, place, and circumstance of your life. These are things that we can't *really* plan for; many of them can strike at any time. In a way, the final stage is a sort of openness to the possibility that things may change.

Getting offered a new job; *losing* your job, achieving a major goal, falling short of one; discovering a loved one is sick and dying; beginning or ending a long-term relationship—these are all examples of the moments I am talking about. Each of these moments offer you the opportunity to reassess what is important—and more importantly, why. At the heart of re-evaluation is the idea that none of us are the people we were five years ago. In five more years, you be even more different still. Life has a flow of its own, and we need to flow with it.

For me, being stuck in the same place isn't any sort of goal. New opportunities and challenges arise every day, but every now and then the world *shifts*. The tectonic plates of the world move under our feet and we need to use the tools and training we have acquired over the years to adjust and make changes wherever they are needed. When these shifts occur, *that* is when you want to re-evaluate.

THE FUTURE IS YOURS—OWN IT

Let's fast forward a little and take a look at a different version of you. You've employed the basics of the AMRAP Mentality to smash some short terms goals. You've also used the AMRAP Mentality to develop a deeper understanding of yourself, your motivations, and your passion—in essence, you've found your *why*. Your why is strong and compelling, and you've honored it with action, sharpening it daily by focusing on the things you can control. You've worked hard...*damn* hard and consistently over weeks, months, and years. Over time, you've come to realize your long-term goals. You've achieved some success. One-by-one you systematically check accomplishments off your list all the while developing a deeper appreciation for the present. Life becomes richer through newly found meaning, perspective, and success. You've successfully unlocked a set of tools to make every second count.

Not bad, right? But certainly not easy. This type of transformation can take years to realize. And the journey toward this kind of long-term enlightenment, despite being undeniably fruitful, can often be a tumultuous mix of success then setback, confidence then doubt, and clarity then confusion. The formula is simple, but the application (or better maybe, the *consistent* application) can be very challenging; however, you must stay the course. Over time, the AMRAP Mentality will become second nature…trust the process.

I've often found that certain key people in my life play a pivotal role in "timing" my re-evaluations. And none are more important and meaningful than Ashley. I've learned so many things from her. In addition to being an incredible wife, she is an incredible mentor, wise counsel, and loyal companion. I attribute much of my success in the sport of fitness and the business of fitness to her. Through highs and lows, Ashley consistently reminds me to remain focused, avoid distraction, and re-evaluate at key moments.

This trend was even evident in our fledgling romance. I first met Ashley in high school, during math class. At the time, we were fourteen, and she was *way* out of my league (still is!). After getting to know each other for a few weeks, we decided to "hang out." I remember going home and telling my mom that I had met the woman I was going to marry. (I've always been steadfast in my convictions.) Funny thing, though…after we dated for two weeks, she dumped me. It was a crushing setback for me at that age, but I would not be deterred. She wanted more out of me, and she wanted to know I was serious about her. I know this sounds silly, but at fourteen Ashley taught me how to not just *talk* about it but *be* about it. I listened, and we have been together ever since.

Large scale, sweeping re-evaluations don't occur often. But that doesn't mean we can dispense with personal re-evaluation entirely. I invest time evaluating how well I'm doing on a daily basis, as well. I look at the big re-evaluation as a sort of sum of all my daily check-ins.

In many ways, it's like your fitness. One workout will not make or break you; however, the sum of your workouts over time will determine your overall fitness, and the path you take. Aside from Ava's illness, only one thing keeps me up at night…this nagging question—*could I be better?*

Could I be a better husband or father? Could I work harder to grow the business? Could I be fitter? Could I be more productive, meaningful, and impactful? *COULD I BE BETTER?* There was a time in my life when this question would cripple me; now, it fuels me. My nightly reflection helps me maintain balance and peak performance across all aspects of my life. *Jason, how did you do today, and could you do better?* Ultimately, the answer is always yes; however, as I've matured, I beat myself up less and coach myself more.

Let's say I neglected workouts due to travel. *Jason, your fitness fuels your energy. It's important you wake up early tomorrow and make time.* Or, if I find conversations with my wife are only surface level because I have been busy with work for the week. *Jason, Ashley is being supportive but it's important that you ask her how she's doing today and plan a date night to reconnect.*

I literally talk to myself. I know this sounds a little weird, but I am telling you…it works! Even if it isn't the self-talk *per se* that I mentioned earlier in the book, a simple conversation with yourself can help you look at things from a different angle and re-evaluate. I figure that if I evaluate myself daily, I minimize the chance for major regrets later on. Life may throw me a few curveballs, but I have peace of mind in knowing that I did the best I could.

WHEN TO GO, AND WHEN TO LET GO

I would be remiss here if I didn't take you back to 2014. My experience at the 2014 Reebok CrossFit Games serves as one of my all-time favorite examples of re-evaluation.

By this point in my competitive career, I felt like a well-oiled machine. I had matured in my ability to assess my performance, both in the moment and over the course of a long trajectory. My most valuable asset in competition had always been this primal *go* switch, the underlying power fueling the *Gotta Go Plan*.

If you and I had to do some work, and you were lined up against me, I would nearly die trying to beat you. I went all-in, all the time. But in 2014, the tides had begun to change for me. I found my *go* button still worked, but that I had to press it a few times before it clicked. I re-evaluated my why going into the Games. Leading up to that year's competition, I had made major life choices that shifted my priorities. I was a family man. I had invested heavily in the growth of my business. But even with all the responsibilities outside of trying to be the fittest person on earth, I tried to give my absolute best in preparing for the Games.

Every time I competed, I tried to leave my heart and soul on the floor. In years past, competing was nearly my entire focus. But in 2014, large shares of my heart and soul were undeniably elsewhere. Ashley and I were blessed with our son Kaden in April of 2014. Now it wasn't just me and the pinnacle of competitive fitness—there was Ashley, Ava, Kaden, NCFIT.

I still gave everything I could summon to that competition. And as the weekend went on, I experienced some terrific performances. I didn't end up winning in 2014, but that's okay. I came in third place and stood very proudly on the podium with both of my children next to me. In 2008, coming in third would have been a failure. In 2014, it was a triumph, because the AMRAP Mentality had enlightened me, and had enabled me to be my best self. I gave my absolute best at every moment of the competition, but more importantly, I owned a clear understanding of my driving force. I had no lingering doubts about my performance or my why. I was truly happy.

As I walked away from the podium at the 2014 CrossFit Games, I felt the fullness of a job well done. I had honored my why through hard work, focus, and more importantly, balance. A major life event had just taken place, and I could feel the world shifting under my feet. I knew I needed to perform a broader evaluation of my competitive career. I also knew this would be a challenging and deeply emotional exercise. It demanded that I ask myself about my passion for the sport and commitment for 2015. Perhaps even scarier…was it time that I hang it up completely?

I know it sounds cliché, but competing in CrossFit was something that I did for *the love of the game*. I always believed that if it ever became about money or fame that it would be time to move on. I could sense that I no longer had the same passion for competing. I still loved the daily workouts, but my enthusiasm for and commitment to vying for the title of the fittest person on earth weren't what they used to be. It was time to change courses.

Ashley and I talked about the decision to stop competing quite a bit. She would support me no matter the outcome; however, I knew deep down that we both desired to spend more time raising our children, building our family, and strengthening our relationship… together. Not while one of us worked out for multiple hours a day.

The answer became clear. If I wanted to continue to perform to the high standards that I had set for myself in all areas of my life—to succeed as the CEO of NCFIT and be the husband and father I wanted to be—then something had to go. So, after finishing as the third fittest man on the planet...I decided to walk away as an individual competitor. In many ways, this was a very easy decision.

DEALING WITH UNANTICIPATED ADVERSITY

Although I had stepped down as an individual competitor, I didn't leave the CrossFit Games entirely, and participated on a team level with the NCFIT crew in 2015. Having the opportunity to compete alongside friends while not enduring the rigors or pressure of individual competition was a wonderful experience, for the most part. I could enjoy training with the team, and also shift more of my energy to my family and business. I learned quite a bit from these 2015 team CrossFit Games, and in many ways, it was a culmination of years working on the AMRAP Mentality.

Our team was in a dominant position, and we had been the favorites going into the competition. Our team was made up of three guys and three girls. Towards the middle of the competition, we were dealt a serious blow when one of our teammates, Miranda, tore her ACL half way through an event. This was of course a very serious injury, and there was no way she could continue. The remaining members had to make a choice: stay in the Games, or drop out.

It actually wasn't up to us, at first, whether or not we stayed in the Games. We spent a pretty on-edge evening waiting for the judges and administrators of the event to decide whether they were going to give us the option to continue. You know what this means—we had to focus on what we could control in order to stay level-headed and in charge of our abilities. Eventually, the word came down: we could stay and compete with five members, if we wanted to.

Of course, we kept going. We threw every tool we had at the rest of the event, and ended up performing significantly better than anyone would have thought. We even managed to beat some full six-person teams! And Miranda has since recovered and started a very successful fitness business of her own. We had to shift gears, make use of the *Gotta Go Plan*, and put everything into it to finish.

I learned many things from this experience, and not just about shifting gears and focusing on what I could control and self-talk. I also started to realize that I couldn't compete like this forever, that the wear and tear on my body was no joke, and that I would have to make some very serious choices about CrossFit and the rest of my life, even beyond retiring as an individual competitor.

Little did I know that in a few short months after these Games, fate would take control and force the greatest re-evaluation of my life. When Ava was diagnosed with leukemia in January 2016, the decisions were simple, yet life altering. Ava's diagnosis and her battle required my full attention. Undoubtedly, I knew it was time to let go of the CrossFit Games and a few other things. I no longer had the time or energy for pettiness, anger, or jealously. Positivity needed to prevail, and I wouldn't allow external negativity to cause me or my daughter any additional stress.

Thinking back now, I often wonder—*would it have been harder to quit when Ava got sick if we had won those Games?* I would have been fired up to keep competing, and it may have been a difficult choice. The way things shook out, though, I ended the 2015 team Games giving serious thought to how my competition affected my family, and at what point I would need to give it up to focus entirely on them and our future together.

I hope that no one ever experiences a diagnosis like Ava's. But life is riddled with uncertainty, and many of you will have to deal with similar, or even worse, situations. I only know what positivity did for me through this entire ordeal. If it was not for positive thinking and focusing on what we could control, I am not sure I would have been strong enough to make it through. My daughter's diagnosis changed our lives on a multitude of levels, and in many ways, it is still impacting life even as I write this book.

RE-EVALUATION IN BUSINESS

Competing on a team at the CrossFit Games offered many lessons that translated well to our business. For years I had focused on being "good" at almost all forms of fitness, but never "great" at any one thing. This is a major component of the CrossFit Games: having a blend of fitness across many areas. For example, if you're too strong, you probably can't run as well. If you are too good of a runner, and you may not be able to do gymnastics well.

In the same way, a business owner or employee trying to do everything on their own…can they *really* get the job done? Perhaps. But focusing on many things allows you to only do everything at a level of effort less than 100%. From my experience, empowering others at work to get the job done allows everyone to be more productive and allows you to focus on what you do best. Team competition allowed me to focus on my strengths more than my weaknesses. This wasn't only more fun for me, but also offered the largest impact to our team. There is a lot of value in working your weaknesses, but in business and team activities, the goal should be to identify strengths. Enhancing the strengths of each participant offers the most benefit to the overall group.

MATURITY, SELF-EVALUATION, AND BRUTAL HONESTY

Letting go of the desire to claim another title was, in part, about becoming an adult. As you grow older, you must identify what you're really about. You have to stand for something, and you have to have a personal code. Everyone's code is different. In my case, I was growing older and had more responsibility, with much higher stakes—a lot higher than when I went on that first road trip to the 2008 CrossFit Games. Ava was very sick, and I needed to devote all of my energy to her immediately. There was no time to train for a fitness competition. Others may find a way to do both, but for me, it was all or nothing. Ava was the priority. Letting go was not only the right thing to do…it was the only thing to do. We were fighting in the biggest competition of our lives against cancer, and we fully intended to win. We *will* win.

This didn't mean I would neglect fitness and health during this time period. I've already mentioned how fitness keeps me sane and helps me cultivate positivity. Maintaining my fitness was a life-giving force. But from that point on in my life, I ditched the obsession with pushing myself to win the CrossFit Games.

A lot of this comes down to honesty, brutal and unrelenting honesty. No matter if you're preforming one of the big re-evaluations that only occurs rarely, or you're taking a daily inventory of your performance, this is a dose of *wake the heck up*. Who you are, what you're doing, what are you all about—does that really matter? Where do you want to go, and do you really want to go there? Are you on the right track, and are you doing everything you can? If so, why aren't you there yet? These questions aren't meant to beat you up or put you down. Even if you haven't reached your goals yet. It's just a pulse check, a splash of cold water to the face, a jolt of energy after a great cup of coffee. You should be fired up about where you're going, and if you're not, maybe it's time to change something.

READER EXERCISE

Mindfulness AMRAP – 30 Minutes:

Set a clock for thirty minutes and perform an honest evaluation (or re-evaluation) of yourself. Take notes. Start by reviewing your why, and then ask yourself the following series of questions and answer with brutal honesty.

- Who are you?
- What are you doing?
- What are you all about?
- Does that really matter?
- Where you do you want to go?
- Do you really want to go there?
- Are you on the right track?
- Are you doing everything you can?
- If so, why aren't you there yet?

Examine your situation and look for opportunities to approve your approach. If necessary, return to your why and re-evaluate your core motivations and desires. Before the thirty minutes expire, set at least two firm dates in the next twelve months for another re-evaluation.

Physical AMRAP – 6 Minutes:

Set a clock for six minutes and do as many burpees as possible in the allotted time.

To perform a burpee, start by standing straight up. Drop to the ground so that your knees and chest touch the ground. Once you have touched the ground, stand (or jump) back up. To complete the rep, jump and clap your hands above your head. Every time you clap, count one rep. Ready? Go!

Jason's Pro-Tip: Sounds awfully familiar doesn't it? This was your first workout in your journey through the AMRAP Mentality. This is the perfect time for a re-evaluation. Remember your score from way back in Chapter One…now go beat it!

CHAPTER 7

LIVING THE AMRAP MENTALITY

I first started working on this book in the final months of 2015. Only a little while later, in January of 2016, Ava was diagnosed with childhood leukemia. Everything changed from that moment, and the book you have just read was not the one I set out to write. What started off as a book about entrepreneurship and fitness became the story of my family, and how the lessons I learned earlier in life helped see us through a tumultuous time.

After two and a half incredibly difficult years, Ava has completed her chemotherapy treatment. That's two-and-a-half years of nerve-wracking hospital visits, of painful lumbar punctures, of pills and masks and countless sleepless nights. As I close this book in the spring of 2018, her first post-treatment blood test has come back—cancer-free.

Today, Ava is a normal kid. She plays with her brother Kaden and can travel with us around the world. For her, the future looks bright and new.

For Ashley and me, the battle is far from over—both when it comes to Ava, and with pediatric cancer in general. The side effects of our daughter's treatment are largely unknown, and we need to remain strong and vigilant. And now that Ava has turned the corner, we can focus on raising money for research, and getting help to other families fighting their own battles.

Along with fighting pediatric cancer, I have been working to set new goals for myself and our company. I have stayed out of the competitive CrossFit scene, but fitness remains a major part of my life. I plan on running a marathon, experiencing new sports, and continuing my journey in jiu jitsu.

NCFIT is growing rapidly, and we have been blessed with an amazing team consisting of world class coaches, friendly and diligent front desk staff, and unbelievably talented ladies and gentlemen behind the scenes who make some real magic happen. Together, we have opened over twenty gyms around the world, from California to Malaysia, and we don't plan on slowing down any time soon! My incredible family, my amazing teammates, and the AMRAP Mentality have helped me succeed beyond my expectations.

THE AMRAP MENTALITY AND YOUR FUTURE

For many people, a solid first exposure to the AMRAP Mentality is going to happen at the gym. Practicing the mentality during a workout is a great way to understand how well it works and, quite honestly, how uncomfortable it can make you. The discomfort is the price you pay for accomplishing more in nine minutes than others might in ninety. But when you get a taste for this and feel the satisfaction, you want to do more of it.

This is not only a tool that will help you live your best life now, it is a powerful way to inoculate your life for the twists and turns of the future. I like to think of it as a hedge against the unforeseen.

Remember a few chapters back when we talked about stress-testing your life? The AMRAP Mentality helps you, even if you don't know it at the time, achieve results now and protect them down the road.

PERSPECTIVE IN ALL THINGS, GOOD AND BAD

Incorporating the AMRAP Mentality isn't just about working hard to make money; it's also about working hard to maintain sustainable relationships. My wife and I have worked hard over the years to keep our relationship as tight as possible. I met Ashley when I was only fourteen; I didn't know who she would be when she was thirty. I'm fortunate to have found the right one, but it hasn't come without hard work and focus. Embracing the AMRAP Mentality while I am with Ashley and the kids has really helped to keep our relationship strong.

Here's one last note on perspective. Each day, I remind myself to be grateful for what we have and the blessings that are right in front of us. For years, and still sometimes today, I'd gotten wrapped up in always wanting more and not appreciating what I already had. Having a drive to work hard and create your own version of success is critical—but your goals and drive shouldn't overshadow your appreciation for the good things right in front of you. It wasn't until Ava's diagnosis and spending so much time in the hospital that I realized just how good we have it. I would never wish the experience we have had on anyone, yet I know our experience hasn't been half as bad as other families'.

Regardless of what you are going through, your current challenge will often feel like the worst thing you've ever faced. Whatever is most immediate often feels the most difficult. Who's to say that having a child with cancer is worse than losing your job? For the person who just lost their job, it might be the worst thing that has happened to them, just like Ava's cancer is the worst thing to happen to Ashley and me. These experiences might be very different, but the AMRAP Mentality can scale to any situation.

It is our duty to support and be there for those who need it, when they need it. Looking at the day with a different perspective changes the entire landscape; it's like looking at the world through a pair of dark sunglasses and then switching to a pair of clear glasses. As we get older, our perspective changes; so much of what we thought was important really isn't. You have a choice each day to look at the world in a positive light or a negative one. I don't know about you, but I choose optimism.

TIME TO PUT THE BOOK DOWN AND GET TO WORK

Let's say you are browsing in an airport bookstore, happen to come across this book, and skip all the way to the last few pages, thinking you will lifehack your way to the answer. Well, I will boil it down for you one last time, but trust me, nothing in life comes as easily as flipping to the end of a book!

If you take one thing away from this book, let it be this: you want greatness, big or small? *Work damn hard at it.* And just when you think you are working hard…WORK HARDER. Work hard in all things, so that when life gets tough you are ready for anything. Make things good now with your hard work, because they might not always be so good.

Understand your motivation, and know your why. Focus on the things you can control. Shift gears when the situation calls for it and re-evaluate after both success and failure. And work hard, from beginning to end.

I have seen so many people work hard for a few weeks or even a solid stretch of a few months, only to drop off. This is the peril of the impatient. The sustained effort is too much for them. Don't be one of those people. Keep working, confident in the knowledge that your relentless commitment and consistency are the keys. Incorporate what you have learned here for as long and as hard as you can.

In the end, the more work you put in and the longer you do it, the better your life will be and the safer your future will be. That's a promise.

It doesn't matter whether or not you are a professional athlete, or already at the top of your game. This works for everyone.

Now it's time to act. Go out there and crush it using the AMRAP Mentality!

APPENDIX

My friends, welcome to the end of this AMRAP. In many ways, it is just the start of your next one. You are now armed with the tools you need to optimize your life. Whether you start by tackling the pile of dishes in the sink, turning up the intensity of your workouts, or diving deeply into your why…the important thing is that you start. Step one is always the most difficult, but I would encourage you not to waste any time. Get right to work.

I am immensely grateful for your consideration and interest in reading this book. I love helping people, and I love seeing them improve their lives both in and out of the gym. I sincerely hope that you have found something that you can use and apply it toward developing and living your why in a great and impactful way. If this book helps even one person better navigate their life or align toward their true north, then it will be a tremendous success.

I will leave you with this…life will get hard, that's an inevitable truth. Life can be a challenging and unpredictable road. There will be times when you will feel beaten down and defeated. It may feel like the entire universe is conspiring against you and that you are destined for failure. Trust me…you are not. You are absolutely capable of greatness. And in those hardest of times, when others might fail or falter, you can rise above. Hold tight to the AMRAP Mentality, remember your why, and focus on what you can control.

Then, when you've got your why locked in…look yourself right in the mirror and say, "Absolutely, I will continue."

I. RECAPPING THE AMRAP MENTALITY

The AMRAP Mentality is a high-performance mindset that embodies five major components. It is the tool I use day in and day out to accomplish goals both large and small. This mindset is a major contributing factor to the success I've earned in competition and in business. It was also one of the most important approaches my wife and I took when figuring out how to manage Ava's battle with leukemia. I hope that you find it meaningful and powerful in your own life. Below you will find a short recap of each facet of the AMRAP Mentality.

Know Your Why

- Your why is the foundation of the AMRAP Mentality. It's the deeper meaning and purpose that drives you. Your why guides your actions and keeps you on course. More than just fuel, a strong why demands intimately knowing and understanding who you are, what you do, and why you do it. Your why may change over time, but one thing remains constant—without a strong why you can get lost, distracted, or end up chasing the wrong things.

Focus on What You Can Control

- In life, business, and competition, things can generally be divided into two categories—what's in your control and what's not in your control. When you boil it down, there are only a few things that are in our control. The good news is that these few things are some of the most powerful: your mindset, actions, reactions, preparation, hard work, and perseverance, among other things. When you take your valuable energy and move it toward focusing on what's out of your control, things can go badly, and fast. This is a weak mindset. You're at the mercy of other people. When it comes down to it, you will be more successful (and happier) by focusing on what you can control.

Work Hard

- Hard, smart work is the currency of the AMRAP Mentality. If you are not ready to put in the work or if you're looking for shortcuts, this mindset is not for you. Roll up your sleeves, ditch the excuses, and start grinding. There's no better way to accomplish your goals than to work really hard. It sounds simple, but a lot of the time we need to stop talking and start doing. So, let's go.

Shift Gears

- Shifting gears in the AMRAP Mentality really means being invested and active in the present. When you're at work, be at work. When you're at home with family, be with your family. When you're working out, work out. Don't be one foot in and one foot out. This is the connection between your body and mind…be all in to your current activity, and when it's time to shift gears to the next thing, be all in there, too. When you're thinking about one thing but doing another you will not achieve optimal results.

AS MANY REPS AS POSSIBLE

Re-Evaluate

- Moments of re-evaluation in the AMRAP Mentality are those times when you need to take a step back to re-examine your why and your focus. These are major milestones, and they usually occur around big changes. Having the ability to re-evaluate is essential and shows a tremendous amount of self-awareness. Over time your goals and your why may change, and that's okay. It's important to stay connected to the world around you and not stay locked into something that no longer is right for you. As the saying goes, timing is everything. It's no different in the AMRAP Mentality…your why when you're twenty may be very different than your why at thirty. Take the time to honor your why by re-examining it over time.

This mindset is not gimmick. It's not a cheap trick, hack, or shortcut. I am not telling you that the AMRAP Mentality will magically transform your life while you lay back and sip frozen margaritas. You will need to work. And for this thing to really fire on all cylinders you will need to be the hardest worker in the room. But you should want it that way. When you learn to enjoy the labor, the success is even sweeter because you've earned it.

II. AMRAP MENTALITY...IN THE GYM

One of the best ways to practice the AMRAP Mentality right now (not tomorrow, not the next day, not on Monday) is through fitness. Fitness plays a huge part in my life. It is a daily ritual for me whether I'm home, on the road, or anywhere in between. I have literally worked out everywhere. In addition to keeping my body ready for whatever life throws my way, it keeps my mind sharp. It helps me gain better perspective and channel my energy. It doesn't matter if you're ten seconds into your fitness journey or a ten-year veteran…you can learn something every time the clock goes from 0:00 to 0:01.

I've put together nine of my favorite workouts below. They are organized both by category (beginner, intermediate, and advanced) and location (at home or hotel). These are places where you will be able to go after it with little to no equipment. If you have access to a gym or if you're lucky enough to have a home gym with more equipment, you can find more workouts by following @nc_fit or @amrapmentality.

Each workout below follows the AMRAP style format. Complete as many rounds or reps of the workout in the allotted time. Please make sure that you respect your current physical condition and warm up properly. If you need to scale or adjust the workout, please do so. It's always better to start off a little slower and work your way up.

Beginner AMRAP Workouts

- Home
  - » AMRAP x 10 minutes
    - ☐ 10 air squats
    - ☐ 5 knee push-ups
    - ☐ 10 knee tucks (lay on back, pull knees to chest)
- Hotel
  - » AMRAP x 10 minutes
    - ☐ 1 minute on the treadmill or bike (moderate pace)
    - ☐ 10 DB press (light)
    - ☐ 5 up/downs (no push-up burpee)

Intermediate AMRAP Workouts

- Home
  - » AMRAP x 15 minutes
    - ☐ 20 alternating lunges
    - ☐ 10 burpees
    - ☐ 20 sit-ups
- Hotel
  - » AMRAP x 15 minutes
    - ☐ 1 minute on the treadmill or bike (hard pace)
    - ☐ 10 DB thruster (moderate)
    - ☐ 10 DB burpees

Advanced AMRAP Workouts

- Home
  - » AMRAP x 20 minutes
    - ☐ 20 jump squats
    - ☐ 15 handstand push-ups
    - ☐ 20 weighted sit-ups
- Hotel
  - » AMRAP x 20 minutes
    - ☐ 1 minute on treadmill or bike (incline sprint)
    - ☐ 10 DB squat cleans (heavy)
    - ☐ 10 DB ground to overhead

For more workouts and workout tips, please follow @amrap-mentality and @jasonkhalipa, both on Instagram. To keep up with what we are doing at NCFIT and to check out some of our class workouts, please follow @nc_fit on Instagram or visit www.nc.fit to learn more. If you're ever in San Jose, drop into one of our gyms and say hi! As always, train smartly and have fun.

III. AMRAP MENTALITY...IN THE KITCHEN

We didn't dive into nutrition in this book, but I wanted to touch on a few quick points regarding food. Nutrition plays an extremely important role in my life and my family's lives. Not only is food the literal fuel for our bodies, but it also provides an opportunity for us to share, bond, and celebrate. It brings us life, joy, and happiness. Focusing on high quality nutrition not only allowed me to excel on the competition floor but also played an integral role in Ava's treatment.

Food can also have a dark side. I can tell you from experience that food can sometimes be used and abused. Sometimes we use food to cope with or hide from our problems. It can be a very dark and lonely spiral. Unfortunately, many people struggle with their relationship with food and will never realize the amazing benefits of sound nutrition.

Nutrition can often be confusing. There's a lot of noise, fad diets, and snake-oil salesmen that get in the way of the truth. The truth about nutrition is powerfully simple. For more about our stance on nutrition, please review NCFIT's Nutrition Philosophy at www.nc.fit/nutrition and follow Ava's Kitchen on Instagram @avas.kitchen.

IV. AMRAP MENTALITY...FOR LIFE

For those more interested in applying the AMRAP Mentality to other types of tasks and goals, there are additional ways to develop the mindset. Here is an example:

Test the AMRAP Mentality on various tasks. Perhaps you need to get a report done at work—one that requires critical thinking and analysis. Rather than peck away at it over the course of an entire day, find a period—say, two hours—when you can lock your door, turn off all distractions, and do it. See how much more quality work you can get done in that single time frame. When the timer goes off, shake it off and recharge by taking a break, such as going for a walk. Then reset the timer for another session.

Apply this exercise to your relationships, to work, to studying for a final exam, even to shoveling the driveway. Each time you do it, you'll get a little better at it. Apply the AMRAP Mentality consistently toward long-term goals, and you'll be unstoppable.

For workouts, podcasts, social media links,
and more information, visit

JASONKHALIPA.COM

ACKNOWLEDGMENTS

To everyone who stepped up big when Ava got sick, including my family, my friends, and our team at NCFIT, I thank you from the bottom of my heart. You made a very challenging situation much easier with your support.

To Mom and Dad for providing me the best examples of commitment and integrity.

To Ashley for always encouraging me to reach my potential. Everything amazing in my life has been because of you.

To Ava and Kaden, you bring a clarity to my life I never had before. Your smile is what I live for, and always will.

To Austin Begeibing for introducing me to the program that changed my life forever.

To my business mentors, including Joe, Minh, Mike, Jerry, and Paul, your support has been unwavering and more impactful than you can imagine.

To all of our current and past NCFIT team members, thank you for being the best group I could ever ask for.

To coach Chris and Adam for the impact you have made on my training and life.

To our NCFIT community for allowing us to do what we love for a living. Thank you!

To Matt Walker for stepping up more times than I can count, you've been a great friend and business partner.

To Matt DellaValle, I'm proud of what we did together on this book. Thank you for all of your help.

To everyone who took the time to read this book, thank you!

Made in the USA
Columbia, SC
30 August 2017